A PRIMER FOR TEACHING ENVIRONMENTAL HISTORY

——— Ten Design Principles ———

Emily Wakild and Michelle K. Berry

DUKE UNIVERSITY PRESS
Durham & London
2018

© 2018 Duke University Press
All rights reserved
Printed in the United States of America
on acid-free paper ∞
Designed by Jennifer Hill
Typeset in Garamond Premier Pro by Tseng Information Systems, Inc.

Library of Congress Cataloging-in-Publication Data
Names: Wakild, Emily, [date] author. | Berry, Michelle K., author.
Title: A primer for teaching environmental history : ten design principles /
Emily Wakild and Michelle K. Berry.
Description: Durham : Duke University Press, 2018. | Series: Design principles
for teaching history | Includes bibliographical references and index.
Identifiers: LCCN 2017049285 (print)
LCCN 2017058072 (ebook)
ISBN 9780822371595 (ebook)
ISBN 9780822371373 (hardcover : alk. paper)
ISBN 9780822371489 (pbk. : alk. paper)
Subjects: LCSH: Human ecology — History — Study and teaching. | Environmental
sciences — Study and teaching. | Environmental education. | Teachers — Training of.
Classification: LCC GF13 (ebook) | LCC GF13 .W35 2018 (print) | DDC 304.2071 — dc23
LC record available at https://lccn.loc.gov/2017049285

Cover art: Corn being unloaded from a combine. Mircea Gherase / Alamy.

A Primer for Teaching Environmental History

DESIGN PRINCIPLES
FOR TEACHING HISTORY
A series edited by Antoinette Burton

For our students: past, present, and future

Contents

Preface: How to Make Use of This Book ix

Acknowledgments xiii

Introduction 1

PART I
APPROACHES
11

One
The Fruit: Into Their Lunch Bags to Teach Relevance and Globalization with Food 13

Two
The Seed: Using Learning Objectives to Build a Course 27

Three
The Hatchet: Wielding Critique to Reconsider Periodization and Place 39

Four
The Llama: Recruiting Animals to Blend Nature and Culture 53

PART II
PATHWAYS
69

Five
The Fields: Science and Going Outside 71

Six
The Land: Sense of Place, Recognition of Spirit 85

Seven
The Power: Energy and Water Regimes 99

PART III
APPLICATIONS
113

Eight
The People: Environmental Justice, Slow Violence,
and Project-Based Learning 115

Nine
The Tools: Using Technology to Enhance Environmental History 131

Ten
The Test: Assessment Methods, Rubrics, and Writing 141

Epilogue 151

Notes 153

Bibliography 163

Index 177

Preface
HOW TO MAKE USE OF THIS BOOK

BECAUSE WHO WE ARE shapes how we learn and the ways we teach, let us begin by introducing ourselves. This book has two authors. We came to teach and understand environmental history on twisting paths in a shared place, the University of Arizona's Department of History. Michelle specializes in the U.S. West and gender history, and Emily focuses on Latin American and world history, but we found ourselves constantly in dialogue over the framing and expression of environmental topics across historiographies. Our personal connections with environmental history reside much deeper. Michelle grew up on a farm in western Colorado, where she heard her parents, neighbors, and fellow farmers remembering times past and debating current political and environmental problems and possibilities. She loved to hike in the deep canyons of the Colorado Plateau and to raft on the white waters of the Colorado and Gunnison rivers, but at any moment it seemed that other people who also loved those activities could take away her brothers' access to traditional hunting grounds. Emily too was the product of the rural Intermountain West, mostly Santa Fe, New Mexico, and the Treasure Valley of Oregon and Idaho, but she was the progeny of bureaucrats rather than farmers. The Treasure Valley, a strangely cosmopolitan agricultural region with Mexican laborers, Japanese farm owners, and large Mormon families, imprinted on

Emily a curiosity about difference. We brought these and other experiences to our training as environmental historians.

After earning our doctorates our paths diverged. Michelle has spent the past nine years teaching in an independent high school in Tucson. Emily worked at an elite southern liberal arts college for five years before taking a position in a western metropolitan state university. These schools have varied curricula, class sizes, and student demographics, which present different opportunities and challenges that have expanded our teaching repertoire. Over a combined twenty-five years of teaching, we've taught U.S., Latin American, and global environmental history courses as well as highly specialized seminars. We have been creative about how to integrate environmental history into more standard courses, such as part of Advanced Placement U.S. History, or as a major component in an introductory undergraduate world history course. This breadth speaks to the opportunities that abound and the ways we've navigated different institutions on the journey of course design. We write this text in tandem and expect that you will hear both of our voices in solo and in harmony throughout.

Two traits brought us together in deep friendship and ultimately allowed us to collaborate on a book about something as personal and individual as teaching. First, we love to laugh, and we both amuse and humor one another routinely. Second, we love to think. When you get down to it, the best teachers do both of those things—often. This book, then, comes from a conviction that teaching, and reading about teaching, should be fun and should stimulate the educator to think. We hope you will find some humor peppered throughout that brings a chuckle or two, and we anticipate that you will find provocative opinions and ideas on pedagogy. What we have written is based on decades of thinking, reading, teaching, laughing, and learning from the choices we have made. At times we attempt to analyze the methods embedded in our examples or reveal the nuances of our opinions and biases; more often we leave that to you. We've endeavored to share successes; lest we seem too optimistic, keep in mind that writing about all our failed lessons would require another full volume. Do not feel compelled to read all of the chapters in order or in one sitting. And don't be discouraged if there is no chapter dedicated to a topic you want to teach—climate change, for example; use the index to locate examples we give on this topic in chapters 3, 7, and 8. By the end of the book we hope you've found some kernels of wisdom and nuggets of inspiration. But most important, we hope you have found much to think about with those colleagues with whom you most love to think.

It may be useful to point out that most of our teaching experiences have been in smallish, face-to-face classrooms of ten to seventy-five students. Most of our classrooms have been relatively flexible discussion-and-lecture combinations with students ages sixteen to twenty-five. We have taught learners of all ages and backgrounds, including English-language learners and students with special needs. Clearly not all of our strategies will work in all places or with all students. Be aware of that as you read. We anticipate our examples based in this setting could be revised by those of you with the desire or expertise to work in other classrooms with other kinds of learners. Great teachers modify their pedagogy based on the needs of the students sitting in front of them, and we provide a range of examples to give you strategies to mold the teaching to your own setting. We do not discuss learning environments of the mega-classroom (those with five hundred and more students), nor have we tackled online teaching or hybrid courses, all of which may be the way of the future. Perhaps some of you have ideas for these kinds of teaching environments that you'd like to share. We would love to hear from you!

This text reflects our choices and competencies. There is no way to provide content ideas from all the places or times about which one could teach environmental history (especially globally). Our areas of expertise in the United States and Latin America are pretty obvious, and we wanted to write about what we know because we thought it important to give you authentic examples rather than ones we borrowed or imagined might work. In addition to showcasing our own knowledge, there are arguments for highlighting the United States and Latin America as geographic regions that merit environmental history approaches. Quite simply, most of the history—environmental and otherwise—taught in the United States is about the United States. The argument for Latin America is the inverse;

Latin America is consistently the region of the world that most befuddles world historians (which is why so many choose to ignore it). Undoubtedly experts on Asia or Africa will have alternative approaches. In sum, our examples could hardly make up a single coherent syllabus because they are not drawn from one course or intended to fit together in a proscribed way. We purposely do not elaborate on or provide syllabi because the point is not to replicate our courses but to think about how to design what will work for you based on your core convictions. We imagine that as you read a detailed example about a lesson on sense of place in the American West it will trigger ideas for a similar lesson using the content with which you are most familiar.

To deal with the mechanics of coauthorship, throughout the book we use varied pronouns—*I*, *you*, and *we*—to narrate our personal and collective journeys in the classroom. We have opted not to use our first names and lay possessive claim to particular stories, strategies, or chapters because in the process of writing, each chapter and most strategies have blended ideas from both of us. We found trying to police the boundaries between our experiences was as futile as cordoning off the United States from Latin America or the rest of the world. Better to let them blend into each other in unexpected ways. This may make the text blurry for some readers, but it allows us to stay true to our collective spirit of expression. If you are desperate to know which author teaches about bananas and which about llamas, email us and we'll tell you.

We approached this book as both a rough guide and a conversation starter. If, by the end, you take out your hatchet and begin to deconstruct our ideas in order to build your own version of environmental history, then we will have succeeded. If, after reading, you feel inspired to plant even one seed in one course about the importance of the environment in the study of the past, then our primary goal will have been achieved. If you do neither of those things, then we will have had a really good time writing a book that made us think, perhaps more than ever before, about our own teaching, and we will cherish that and all the laughter that journey brought to our friendship.

Acknowledgments

THIS BOOK DISTILLS decades of classroom experience into a uniform discussion. It is not the product of one or two voices but a cacophony of cumulative contributions from students, colleagues, mentors, and friends. The book could never have been written without Antoinette Burton's invitation to put our teaching practice into prose. She is a force for all that is good in the discipline of history, and her forward-looking role as both guide and inspiration provided us an outlet for a very different but deeply necessary kind of scholarly writing. We are very thankful to the other authors in the series, and several insightful graduate students from the University of Illinois, for critically and carefully reading the initial manuscript draft. The University of Illinois and Duke University Press generously sponsored the workshop around our initial draft, which made all the difference. Incredible external reviewers gave particularly insightful critiques about organization, content, and structure as well as ideas for evening out the tone. We gratefully acknowledge all their wisdom.

Emily: Teaching is always a collaborative endeavor. In this spirit I would like to acknowledge the importance of many conversations with other teachers and scholars similarly committed to excellent teaching, including Amanda Ashley, Bill Beezley, Lisa Blee, Lisa Brady, Chris Boyer, Mark Carey, José Augusto Drummond, Sterling Evans, Dee Dee Delongpre

Johnson, Jennifer Jopp, Lori Hausegger, Kevin Gosner, Claudia Leal, Nick Miller, Katherine Morrissey, Monique O'Connell, Germán Palacio, Nate Plageman, Bob Reinhardt, Myrna Santiago, Bill Smaldone, Miles Silman, Rebecca Som Castellano, Doug Weiner, David Wilkins, and especially the late B. J. Barickman. Nick Miller and Lisa Brady have been reliable, helpful, weekly voices of reason who improved the original proposal and many chapters. Darren Speece offered great suggestions on an early draft of the manuscript. I had the privilege of working as a teaching assistant in Michelle's environmental history classroom in 2004, an experience that expanded an already strong friendship and solidified our relationship as coteachers. I can't imagine writing a book like this with anyone else, and I continue to learn so much from her.

Several institutions have supported this project both directly and indirectly. The excellent faculty members in the departments of history at the University of Arizona, Wake Forest University, and Boise State University have provided me great latitude in designing courses and experimenting with teaching. The students in each of those experiments deserve credit as well; one can only hope that some of the intended lessons resonated. A National Endowment for the Humanities Fellowship for 2015–16 provided me ample time to write and organize the initial draft, and the Arts and Humanities Institute of Boise State University provided a lovely office with a view of the Boise River in Yanke Research Park. Familial support is an underappreciated but essential component of scholarly writing and effective teaching. Geoff and Debbie Middaugh and Chuck and Susie Wakild showed interest in and support of this project in many ways. Most of all, Eric Wakild is an inspiring teacher in his own right, especially of the two small humans we brought into the world while this project gestated. Ray and Charlotte have distracted me from writing more than anything, but it is my greatest hope that by teaching environmental history we might leave them a better earth.

Michelle: I would like, first, to acknowledge Emily Wakild, whose constant camaraderie in teaching and soul sister friendship has been a steadfast inspiration for going on fifteen years and without whom I would have never worked on this book.

ACKNOWLEDGMENTS

I must also thank my students. Our intellectual journeys together are some of my most cherished memories. I appreciate those willing adventurers who understood just where I wanted to go and happily joined me, even if it seemed crazy. You were my north stars, and everything I did in the classroom and in the summer prep hours, I did for you. But I also appreciate the skeptics. You know who you are; you made me reflect and revise my practice to try to convince you to read more, write happily, and think willingly. Thank you all for making me a better teacher.

The Department of History at the University of Arizona has for many years been my muse for all things scholarly. Even as I traveled to the east side of town for nearly a decade of high school teaching, UofA was home. The years I spent in the classroom at St. Gregory College Preparatory School are what informed much of the experience I have shared here. To the administrators, such as Jonathan Martin, who encouraged academic autonomy and innovative, rigorous instructional practices, and to my many colleagues who shared my passion for teaching, I will be forever grateful.

In graduate school, teaching is not always the emphasis, and those who spend time on their craft are often encouraged to focus on their research instead, since that is what will ultimately land "a job." But my experience at the University of Arizona could not have been more different thanks to my mentors and colleagues, who loved teaching as much as I did and encouraged me in what I considered to be my vocation. Among those, and in no particular order, are Karen Anderson, Katherine Morrissey, Sally Deutsch, Reeve Huston, Kevin Gosner, Steve Johnstone, Alison Futrell, B. J. Barickman, Doug Weiner, Linda Darling, Luke Ryan, and Jodie Kreider. At St. Gregory I was honored to work with educators (including many coaches) who understood and privileged student-centeredness to such an extent that it forced me to be a better teacher. Among them were Paul Baranowski, Kate Oubre, Dan and Elizabeth Young, Vic Acuna, Ashley David, Shannon Smith, and Angela Earnhart. I was also fortunate to go to the best teaching undergraduate school in the country (The Colorado College), and I remain forever grateful to Anne Hyde and Doug Monroy for all they taught me.

ACKNOWLEDGMENTS

Not long ago I read an article shared by Karen Anderson arguing that those whose work is their vocation tend to burn out sooner than those who consider work to be just work. I fear I might have fallen into that category were it not for my friends and family. My parents have always encouraged my scholarship and general nerdiness. Now my dad can stop asking, "How's the book?" My brother, Mike, my nephews, Mark and Matthew, and my incredible in-laws (Kay, Rich, Joe, Merc, Hayden, Gabby, Carlene) all humor my strange obsession with education and even encourage it. My furbabies remind me that all you *really* need in life is some exercise, good food, and a cuddle. My friends have kept me grounded during fifteen years in the classroom with good humor, good wine, and great conversation (often about teaching). I am especially grateful for Adam Geary, Megan Mulligan, Leslie Kim (and family), Emily Brott, Chris Martin, Christine Thornton, Brian Henry, Melissa and David Cornell, Emma Finkelstein, Alyssa Metcalf, Ariella Faitelson, and Matt and Steph Teller.

Most of all, I am grateful for Anne Stolcis, my partner for twenty-five years. She not only encouraged me throughout this project; she actually thinks teaching is cool and has allowed me to continually strive to perfect my passion. Life with her is beautiful.

Introduction

ENVIRONMENTAL HISTORY has arrived. It has moved out of the periphery and into the mainstream. Over the past forty years the number of history departments employing an environmental historian increased from under 4 percent to more than 40 percent.[1] Strenuous debates and scores of agonizing definitions have been written to explain what environmental history is and why it matters. Fewer, though, have made a case for how it can be taught. This book makes that case.

Students are hungry for humanistic approaches to scientifically driven problems. This is especially true because the humanities can be inviting, flexible, and experimental rather than made inaccessible by the obligatory mastery of quantitative theories.[2] One major advantage of environmental history is that it deals with a tangible past and present, which makes it a remarkable tool for understanding society.[3] Environmental history can appeal to a wide array of students precisely because it provides an expansive and creative approach that is grounded in the material world students observe changing before their eyes. Recognizing geological forces, climatological phenomena, and other organisms in our reconstructions of the human past will provide a more complete picture of how, when, and why humans have been able to tell their own stories and forge their own societies nestled within and shaped by environmental constraints and possibilities.

INTRODUCTION

Humanists have spent decades contextualizing and explaining the varied human experiences across racial, ethnic, class, gender, generational, and educational divides. But we can do more. Neglecting environmental topics is no longer ethically reasonable. To leave the environment out of history is to imagine that humans live in a world different from this one. This might be an appropriate exercise for the future, but it hardly does justice to the past. Whether or not we are headed for an environmental or nonhuman "turn" that shifts substantive theoretical research on par with the "cultural turn" of the 1980s–1990s remains to be seen.[4] But a shift of attention and interest toward the relationships between humans and nonhumans captures rising concern from various directions. In order to get students to think about what it means—in the past, present, and future—to expand our understanding of humanity and to consider that humans are not alone, we must be deliberate in our choices and provocative in our planning.

Here you will find ample discussion of what course design means and why it matters; you won't find an overview of historiography. This is because we feel many historians talk much about the latter to the exclusion of the former. Consider one thing that is universal in any history department: historians love to talk about books. The most common response from a professor asked how to teach something is a list of what to read. Although it is a start, such bibliophilia can falsely substitute for a real conversation about the mechanics of teaching and learning. Most historians might willingly discuss books at happy hour, but teaching methods are more typical topics for faculty meetings and hierarchical evaluations. There are many reasons for this, but one of them is that few historians write about their own teaching experiences. We're even less likely to write about pedagogy as a process or shared endeavor. Yet methods, assessments, pacing, questioning, and organization govern how our favorite books reach students and what they learn to do with them. Because of this, we aim to convene a conversation about *how*—not merely what or why—teaching environmental history can be done. More than the books you assign or the content you cover, how you put readings and content together and what you have students do with them create a syllabus and guide a course.

INTRODUCTION

With that in mind, this book has two interrelated goals. We aim, first, to provide strategies for designing a new course on environmental history and, second, to deliver ideas for infusing environmental history into existing courses. You are the only expert on your courses, your curriculum, and your constraints; only you can decide the appropriate approach. We can offer stimulus, inspiration, and a conversation about how and why to design purposefully. We suggest very few and very basic definitions and overviews of environmental history as a scholarly field. If you are looking to get up to speed with the latest research, we suggest you read the terrific journal *Environmental History* or peruse the many historiographic essays and debates found in other places.[5] In addition you will glean various texts and arguments from our discussions of teaching materials. No one resource or scholar epitomizes how environmental history must be done — the paths are plentiful.

The need for specific discussions of technique is made more acute by the abundance of tangential advice. As is true of so much in our modern world, ample materials are readily available — syllabi, textbooks, primary source readers, edited collections — but if you don't know what you are looking for or why you need it, it is hard to locate the appropriate scholarship. We attempt to sidestep these issues by sharing our experiences planning, teaching, and reflecting with colleagues. We explain specific models and assignments to reveal the convictions that shape our choices and expose the ways these have played out in our classrooms. We believe that a systematic approach to planning a course delivers purposeful instruction, which in turn allows students to harness the past as a perspective that goes beyond a single book or a solitary course. The remainder of this introduction provides some ways of approaching the sprawling field and makes a case for how historical methods are central to teaching it.

Environmental history is the history of human interactions with the rest of the natural world. This comes in many forms, scales, and styles. It has no geographical or temporal preference; it can be as particular as a gray squirrel or as expansive as a petroleum-fueled economy.[6] Ellen Stroud has pointed out that environmental history's claim to significance is its expansive materiality. She argues that the environment is not equivalent to race or gender as a *category* of analysis but instead forms the world in which all categories of analysis exist.[7] As such, environmental history can be a metahistory for synthesizing all histories; most important, it suggests that our understandings of the past are incomplete without factoring in how nonhuman forces and actors have played a role in the human story.

Environmental history shares space with environmental studies and natural history, but it more carefully links our collective place in many kinds of nature with changes and continuities across social, political, cultural, and economic divides. The most common assumption about environmental history is that it tells the story of how people have tried to defend something called the environment with legislation, nature reserves, protests, or other tactics. This greatly oversimplifies the field with too much focus on the human side of things. But neither is the objective exclusively nature-focused. While natural history might describe the life and habits of salmon, environmental history would explain as well how salmon have been caught, eaten, and conceptualized by humans.[8] Environmentalist studies and natural history each contribute content to the practice of environmental history, but neither alone provides the full range of possibilities.

The current sophistication of environmental history comes from the fact it is both an old and a new field. The historical field, as a source of research, courses, and training, has been around for about forty years, but the idea of examining nature and culture as intertwined is much older. Two broad interpretations—progress and decline—characterized much early work. Researchers in many fields, especially geographers, anthropologists, and some historians, included the environment in history as part of a progressive interpretation of the human past that largely envisioned civilization as a steady process of learning to control and manage nature, first through agriculture, then cities, industries, and today's technologies. In this view the solution to environmental challenges would likely emerge from innovation and progress, as it supposedly had before. The contrarian view, declension, instead saw modernization as a fall from grace. In a declensionist view, agriculture marked the departure from harmony leading to further pitfalls and exponential crises. Both approaches are fraught with simplistic and ahistorical problems: both assume we're all in the human project together, both overlook backward drift and catastrophes, and both ignore the fact there is no single harmonious point to reach or return to.[9] Rather than reconstruct them, knowing these approaches exist and have shaped decision making can provide a structural backbone for a course. Identifying progressive and declensionist narratives allows the emergence of more satisfying tales, such as those of change and adaptation.

If progress and decline at first limited the environmental stories that were told, several additional pitfalls have clouded environmental history's approach or deterred otherwise critical historians from examining nature's past. Many historians conflated the idea of paying attention to nonhuman nature as ceding explanatory power to geographic, climatic, or genetic forces. Such determinism had a formative—and understandably worrisome—role in linking eugenics with the environment. This is not the line of inquiry advocated by the field. Deterministic views posit that humanity is locked into fated ends, but environmental history reveals quite the opposite. A perennial challenge of environmental history is to examine the ways environmental forces are consequential but not all-powerful. Indeed rather than imagine that certain peoples are uniquely suited to particular climates, environmental histories unravel the specific ways geography, climate, and natural processes shape and are shaped by cultures.[10] More often than not, these dynamics shift our expectations rather than confirm our suppositions.

As much as avoiding determinism, environmental history avoids the assumption of universal values toward aspects of nature. For instance, before 1700 forests in Europe and the Americas were commonly viewed as better cleared to make room for farmland. By 1900 forests were better replanted, to recover other benefits. Over these two to three centuries, forests went from foes to friends, which affected other populations, such as sheep and shepherds that used meadows instead of forests. This is not to say that environmental history cannot guide value judgments but that they should be transparent: neither sheep nor trees nor humans are unilaterally good or bad. Similarly the notion of a pristine or untouched nature, usually imagined to exist before Europeans arrived in the Americas, sets up a false dichotomy of good humans and bad humans, harmonious nature and disturbed nature. Neither nature nor humanity forms a stable unit, but when and why such harmony has been perceived are topics of historical interest.

The pitfalls might seem daunting, but the promises of environmental history loom even larger. By viewing nature and culture as intertwined in a long-term relationship, we can see the ways they both change dynamically, mutually, and unevenly. Such a relationship allows us to envision the intimate connections between external and internal nature — meaning humans are biological organisms but also cultural products. For example, Nancy Langston has shown that on the most basic level our private bodily fluids do not end with us but instead make it into waters we share with other creatures.[11] She historicizes how the hormones in women's urine have affected other species — producing pregnant male fish, small-penis alligators, spermless panthers, and hermaphrodite polar bears — and she asks how these bizarre problems with gender and reproductive health link humans and wildlife. What we eat, drink, and excrete connects us to our specific human culture and also to the biological systems of the planet. In such ways environmental history promises more complete stories because it draws upon other types of history, from the categories of race, class, gender, age, occupation, and experience of social history to cultural history's focus on material objects, sites of meaning, and concentrations of power and access.

Environmental historians reach promiscuously across wider disciplinary divides into ecology, literature, policy, and more. We must both deal with the ecological consequences of human activity and introduce ecology as an explanation for historical processes. Histories are often conveniently bifurcated along invented national boundaries that overlook the ways natural processes go beyond them. Transcending the nation-state provides an open invitation for global connections. *Global* cannot imply *comprehensive*, but some processes—such as air pollution, biodiversity loss, and ocean fishing—come into focus only with larger lenses.

The complexity of environmental history is substantiated by an ever-increasing field of study. Undoubtedly, from its origins in the U.S. West to its global reach to and separate origins within Europe, Latin America, Africa, and Asia, the field harbors critical imbalances in gender, geography, and training that have repercussions if we want to inspire a new generation of students to engage with the field.[12] We attempt to mediate some of these concerns by using more recent work rather than classics in some cases and by providing suggestions rather than full-fledged examples of places we know less well. We reiterate our caveat that this book makes no claims to capture the entirety of the exciting global span of environmental history or to provide more than a sampling of possible lessons, examples, and models. In particular we welcome scholars of Asia, Africa, and Europe to offer up their own best practices and perhaps even a companion volume.

Rather than simply being something to know, environmental history, like all good history, makes the past come alive because it provides a focused approach for engagement. Other disciplines that study the environment—from biology and geography to literature and anthropology—do not necessarily understand historical methods, in part because we historians do not articulate and explain our methods enough or empower our students to do so. We feel the best way to get students interested in and practicing environmental history is to give them the tools to do it. This involves discussing the basic level of what we do, especially showing students how to find sources, how to take them apart, and how to put them back together again in a cohesive narrative (and consider what it means to do so). Locating, contextualizing, and corroborating evidence for analysis is the first step to historicizing a society or an event, and this process itself can be deeply revealing of the contours of historical research and study. Environmental historians might cast their search for sources broadly to include cultural as well as natural archives as they seek to understand landscape change or species evolution in tandem with exploration and colonization, for instance. They could turn to dendrochronologists' charts of tree rings to understand drought or the color and shading of oil paintings to contextualize experiences of prolonged winter. Wherever they look, environmental historians aim to listen to people listening to nature.

Once sources are identified — which alone is a daunting task — historical methods get trickier. Identifying various perspectives captures the intricacy of the past and opens up avenues of inquiry that encourage students to empathize with the lives of people who are different from them. Sensitivity to the potential of understanding past lived experiences creates the space and flexibility for students to make connections across time, place, and discipline. Close textual analysis and deeply nuanced cultural and linguistic readings of sources (visual, textual, or data-centered) teach students how to read all over again. Exercises that practice these habits build the tools to deconstruct knowledge students already have and provide insights to see how various fragments might fit together in another way.

Students of history learn and practice how to situate and make relevant multiple perspectives. They are required to make sense out of a flood of stories — droplets of human experience that slip through quantitative models or set loose overly rigid comparisons. Historians see human motive in the texts they read and the stories they hear, and they seek veracity from innuendo and falsehood. In piecing together coherent explanations for what has already happened, students learn to build a narrative that embraces complexity while simultaneously searching for clarity and coherence. One student might see dramatic change over time while another picks out a strand of continuity. Telling the story as they see it and basing that story on reliable sources is both an iterative and an interrogative process. And the process relies on slow thinking, extensive questioning, and deep deliberation in order to make choices and balance opinions to form more complete stories. Asked what skills history teaches, many of us might suggest analytical thinking and clear writing. These are perhaps the most marketable end products, but getting to them involves many earlier steps that should be intentionally targeted in our courses.

The chapters that follow are organized into three sections. Part I, "Approaches," provides four strategies for navigating your way into environmental history: a piece of fruit, a seed, a hatchet, and a llama. We begin with *the fruit* as an ordinary and familiar centerpiece for asking questions and building connections. By examining several ways histories of food can make environmental history relevant as an authentic part of daily life, fruit provides students a tangible conduit between their bodies and the natural world. The second, *the seed*, offers ideas for fostering complexity in content and narratives, ensuring that your course does more than point out environmental use and abuse by making students aware of progressive and declensionist perspectives. The chapter gives suggestions for clarifying language and setting up roundtable discussions. Taking timelines as the structural framework, *the hatchet* cuts into the traditional scaffolding of old and new courses to make room for environmental perspectives. Considering both periodization and place, it discusses questioning as a form of building context and climate change as a topic to break down existing narratives. The fourth example uses animals, starting with *the llama*, as entry points into a course on human relationships with nature. Exploring topics and techniques suited to this unconventional historical subject, the chapter seeks to examine ways of blending nature and culture by paying attention to other organisms.

Part II, "Pathways," may inspire you to consider old topics anew. The first pathway, *the fields*, leads into the wider world, meaning both places outside the classroom doors and various other fields, especially scientific disciplines. This literal and figurative field trip helps us to articulate ways of using science and science writing in history courses. Next, in *the land*, we consider how our senses of place awaken deep connections that shape people's choices at critical historical junctures. In the final example from this section, *the power*, we examine two of the richest threads of resource use in environmental history: energy and water. Either topic could provide an exciting stand-alone course, but we examine their intertwined nature and history as a productive pathway for students.

Part III, "Applications," steps outside specific examples to address three of the larger issues hovering over our classrooms: diversity, technology, and testing. Inequality is a theme in many of the examples of this book, but in chapter 8 we explicitly examine environmental justice, that is, examples of how and why certain groups, especially the poor, people of color, and women, have suffered disproportionately from environmental degradation. This topic has both methodological and thematic implications. Environmental justice allows us to explore, through individual lives, how environmental history is not just about nature but is also about power differences among human communities. Project-based learning emerges as a holistic way of getting students to grapple with inequality, and the examples and activities demonstrate our concern for applying content to students' current lives and civic choices. The ninth chapter, dedicated to *the tools*, considers various ways of planning for and teaching with technology as both a subject of environmental history and an application embedded in our courses. And in chapter 10, on *the test*, we discuss assessment as part of the design of a course. We suggest that abandoning the test and embracing creative assignments might just improve student learning.

PART I

Approaches

NOW THAT YOU HAVE a sense of our conception of environmental history and our view of historical methods, we provide examples from our classrooms. We endeavor to reach students where they are and bring them into environmental history by providing multiple points of entry. Each chapter in this section explains an approach or a specific device that also serves as a metaphor for the intellectual work of course design: fruit, seeds, a hatchet, and animals. Throughout these chapters we suggest places, people, and products that you can use to provide compelling evidence of humans' changing relationships with nature and of nature's role in history. By exposing our own choices and placing them in the context of building a syllabus, assignment, or lesson, we hope to free you from the enormity of environmental history and inspire you to explore its potential.

Chapter One

The Fruit

INTO THEIR LUNCH BAGS TO TEACH RELEVANCE
AND GLOBALIZATION WITH FOOD

"BUT I DON'T LIKE NATURE *at all*. Bugs scare me," proclaimed a student who was deciding whether or not to take my U.S. Environmental History course. Another said, "I'm so *not* outdoorsy," and a third said, "I am more interested in economics and science." For a student who lives in a city of over a million people in the Sonoran Desert that is hot and prickly much of the year, the first student's sentiment didn't surprise me, nor did the notion that one must be a hiker or a tree hugger in order to dig environmental history. The student who believed that environmental history is separate from the study of economics and science, however, astonished me. That sentiment reminded me of how little our students know about the importance of the earth and its processes in the larger scheme of things. Explaining and drumming up interest in the topic is one of the greatest challenges for teachers of environmental history.

This chapter introduces a variety of ideas for how to make the case to students that studying environmental history is relevant to them. We should think about relevance in another way as well: the relevance the discipline has for revolutionary teaching. bell hooks has argued that the transformative potential of education is its power to encourage democratic decision making in the future.[1] In order to achieve that noble end, one must teach the skills students need to engage deeply in democratic processes. Perhaps not surprisingly, progressive pedagogy tells us that skills should be at the center of what we teach, even more so than content, if we are to affect a future for our students in which they do not simply receive information and recite it but are empowered to critically think about information, communicate those thoughts, and solve problems on a daily basis. This, then, is the second place where the relevance of environmental history must be understood: by us, the teachers. Environmental history's relevance in students' daily lives gives it the potential to facilitate the essential acquisition of skills such as communication, creative problem solving, critical thinking, and collaboration. The study of environmental history requires multidisciplinary understandings and perspectives, and therefore it applies to every facet of real life. It is this last truth that must be engagingly communicated to students.

One way to make environmental history readily relevant to our students is through a discussion of food. Our students live in a world that prizes the fast. Google provides answers in a nanosecond. Amazon can complete an order in less than two hours from purchase to delivery. Music and mobile apps download onto devices on demand. In addition our students live in a global world — at least in terms of their technological exposure. They know, even if they don't always take advantage of it, that fast food is there waiting at McDonald's at all hours and that a wide variety of cuisine peppers their culinary landscape. But when our students order the Big Mac, they don't see cows, corn, water, or the long global history of husbandry that is present in the "all-beef" patty. Students, especially urban students (who we can assume are upward of 75 percent of those in our classrooms), often do not understand the *slow*, painstaking, and often transnational processes that go into growing and harvesting that food. Introducing students, first, to the agro reality of their food is an important step in asking them to trace the history of their lunch so they can more easily grasp that environmental history transcends a seemingly simple study of trees and bugs.

The context of food is, obviously, agriculture, and the study of agriculture can be as riveting as watching corn grow. Assigning common general readings or film viewings or both is an excellent way to begin a foray into food history. The benefit of connecting academic study to the real world is that it opens up significantly more engaging sources for students, especially through journalistic and documentary texts. In the case of food, no author is better for this task than Michael Pollan. The erudition and accessibility of his writing make him a great choice for students at all levels. He talks about agriculture (literally the cultivation of fields) and plant evolution in a way that titillates rather than bores and that immediately connects the eon-long practice of human cultivation of plants to the present day. He also subtly but consistently shows how food has global, environmental consequences.

Consider this, from his introduction to *The Botany of Desire*:

> The DNA of that tulip there, the ivory one with the petals attenuated like sabers, contains detailed instructions on how best to catch the eye not of a bee but of an Ottoman Turk; it has something to tell us about that age's idea of beauty. Likewise, every Russet Burbank potato holds within it a treatise about our industrial food chain — and our taste for long, perfectly golden french fries.... We have spent the last few thousand years remaking these species through artificial selection, transforming a tiny, toxic root node into a fat, nourishing potato and a short, unprepossessing wildflower into a tall, ravishing tulip. What is much less obvious, at least to us, is that these plants have, at the same time, been going about the business of remaking us.[2]

Pollan is not just an approachable writer but a prolific one; in addition to his published book-length works, he has an impressive online presence. He has several advocacy columns published online, and PBS has produced an excellent documentary, called *The Botany of Desire*, on his work. An instructor could use all of these sources in what I call a "sources in the round" discussion. In this assignment students access different kinds of sources (in small groups) and come to class prepared to highlight the content of the sources (What was learned?) and to discuss the efficacy of the source to communicate the information (How did we learn it?). Is a documentary film more effective than a book chapter? What gets left out of each? Is there enough information in Pollan's columns in the *New York Times* to fully inform the reader? Thus one can assign a documentary, an excerpt from one of his book chapters, and a sampling of his food advocacy blogs early in the semester and begin a robust conversation about the merits and drawbacks of certain kinds of sources *while also* introducing students to the importance of their lunch and the relevance of environmental history. Of course assigning a primary source from a planter in the nineteenth-century American South connecting the cotton plant to its slave caretakers is important as well, but not, perhaps, as effective in the early days of the course. In the first days establishing relevance by introducing students to the timeliness (versus the timelessness) of the discipline is crucial.

Once I have introduced students to agriculture and food generally, it is time to ask them to get personal. The personalization of history can be a daunting task in a gender history class or in a study of whiteness. Such personalization can be sensitive material for students who are not used to being asked to think about their own identity in connection with oppression and domination. Thankfully in the early days of an environmental history class, this personalization comes a bit more easily. One approach is to pick an item of food and ask students to think critically about what it takes to grow and harvest it and what it takes for it to be sitting on their lunch table. Take, for example, the ubiquitous banana.

The banana epitomizes the interdisciplinary relevance, current applicability, and global interconnectedness of environmental history largely because people love it. According to the U.S. Department of Agriculture, the banana is America's most popular fruit; in the year 2010 each American on average consumed ten pounds of bananas.[3] Yet it is not cultivated in the United States. Thus, immediately, a study of the banana as a discrete research unit on globalization or as an introductory lesson on relevance fits in all kinds of courses. The banana's cultural, political, and ecological legacies are vast; the challenge lies in making the sweeping content accessible for students and manageable for the instructor. I usually start by playing the catchy tune "Yes! We Have No Bananas," first released in 1922 and likely inspired by a shortage of bananas in grocery stores in New York City. The shortage resulted from the Panama Blight, which caused billions of dollars of damage to the global banana export business in the early twentieth century. By the 1950s the entire transnational business of banana cultivation and consumption was undermined because of the fungus. And there's that ditty, just begging for critical analysis. Playing the song as the introduction to the banana lesson piques the interest of students. Asking them to guess why the Greek grocer would be out of bananas in 1922 can get the discussion going. Hopefully the students will come up with a variety of reasons: the delivery truck didn't come, the bananas didn't grow, someone in the store forgot to order the bananas, the bananas sold out, and so on. With each new idea about why the grocer is out of bananas, the class is building and thinking more deeply about the global story of the fruit.

By 1922 the banana was a global commodity. Helping students to understand that *all* environmental history (including food history) is global in nature should be an important objective for any environmental history course. The different zones of the earth have been ecologically connected for time immemorial and linked through human culture for half a millennium, but is that the same as the process of globalization? Just what is globalization? This is one topic where posing a question is almost more important and certainly more provocative than providing a definition. Student responses will include ideas about interconnectedness, cultural and economic exchanges, and political and ideological interactions. In other words, globalization is a trendy way of talking about the core of what historians analyze: flows, networks, outlooks, assemblages, and nodes of interaction taking place across ethnic, national, cultural, and social boundaries. One way to historicize current discussions about globalization is to center the processes at work and link them to environmental opportunities and constraints. Food, particularly the banana, is an excellent conduit to do just that.

Global capitalist agriculture as a regime of domination is represented in the environmental history of the popularization and commoditization of the Big Mike and Cavendish varietals of banana. What an opportunity for a world history course on trade or in AP U.S. History to zero in on trade globalization using a specific food commodity like the banana's impressive rise in the Gilded Age. If you are required to teach an economics strand, you can weave in a bit of environmental history with the banana to introduce students to ideas about consumerism and the fundamental linkages between supply and demand. Labor and capital, natural resource exploitation through the use of fossil fuels, and the expansion of global trade all unite there, in the delicious fruits traveling inside waxy boxes to the grocery store bins. (Heck, you can even have students think about the ways the environment exists in the waxy box as well!)

Since all bananas are related in some way (they are, in the loosest sense of the word, cloned), the banana can also help students begin to grapple with the meanings of *nature* and *natural*. This is a particularly important definitional process to undertake early in a stand-alone course on environmental history. What does it mean to be natural? If we define nature as untouched by humanity, is there any nature left on earth? Surely not on the banana plantations! The banana rose to popularity and prominence in the late nineteenth and early twentieth centuries through intentional marketing of the United Fruit Company (UFC) as well as the serendipitous health craze that swept the United States. This rise demonstrates that environmental history necessarily includes research on agriculture, globalization, and culture, and that so many current economic, political, and social justice issues have relevance to and can be best understood as rooted in an environmental and ecological past.

For example, the Cavendish banana, the most ubiquitous variety and the most heavily traded, is a human construction. After the Gros Michel, also called Big Mike, succumbed to Panama Disease (*Fusarium oxysporum*), the Cavendish was cultivated through cloning techniques, first in a lab and then in the field. It then came to stand in for the Big Mike. This part of the banana's history helps students to understand that farming is human cultivation but also highly dependent on a nature that is independent from human manipulation. This subtopic opens opportunities for debate on genetic engineering (genetically modified organisms, GMOs) as well as the pros and cons of monoculture versus polyculture and of industrial agriculture versus premodern (or even organic) agriculture. The eventual dramatic exploitation of rain forests can be brought to bear on these conversations as well and can be used to introduce students to the ways this one lunch bag commodity may be partially responsible for climate change the world over.

Because students often associate environmental history with those yucky bugs and with trees (how *boring*, yawn), it is early in the course that we have the chance to show them that environmental history is not just about nature; it is a truly transdisciplinary subject that should inform and complicate our understandings of capitalism, imperialism, and industrialization. One entrée into this point is to ask them to think about their culture of consumption. Keeping with the banana, you might ask students to literally or imaginatively travel to the world of fashion. Begin with a field trip to the multinational clothing store Banana Republic. Utilizing students' social media tools is one way to get them somewhere without having to actually travel. For instance, Banana Republic has a very active Instagram account. Have your students follow the company's posts and think critically about the messages and images they find there. Once students know a little bit about the banana and its political ecology, they should be ready to wonder about the reasons behind naming a company after such an exploitative notion and what environmental costs are associated with the products depicted on Banana Republic's Instagram.[4]

The discussion of the ways in which economic globalization and environmental consumerism and labor exploitation work hand in glove can then begin in earnest. You can spend time on the cultivation of cotton, rayon, polyester, or any other of the myriad raw materials of those cute shirts hanging on the shelves of that oh-so-aptly-named shop. This will offer the students and you the opportunity to think too about the feminization of poverty and the gendering of work. The very symbol of the Chiquita girl opens a perfect opportunity to discuss the conflation of environment, cultivation, and the gendered division of labor. As Carolyn

Merchant begs us to remember, "a sensitivity to gender enriches environmental history" because women have related to and been conflated with nonhuman nature differently from men.[5] The association of the Eve-like Chiquita image with nature in order to sell the socially constructed banana can offer a tangible and discrete symbol to students as they begin thinking about the connections among nature, culture, modes of production, and gender relations.

Other social relations and conflicts are embedded into the flesh of the mighty banana. An investigation of big capital and its social dominance through agriculture is low-hanging fruit for a unit or a project focused on the UFC and its connections to racism, migratory labor relations, democratic revolutions, the slow food movement, and more.[6] Our students live in a world where, if they are paying attention, democratic social movements litter the global landscape, debates about immigration and racism are omnipresent, and foodie culture is pervasive. Again social media can serve as an instantly gratifying hook for our students. Ask students to research one of these issues and find one type of social media activists have used to characterize the cause. Why does that cause lend itself to that particular kind of social media? Is slow food more effectively publicized through the imagery that can be created on Instagram? Would a food revolution benefit more from having a twenty-four-hour Twitter feed? Why might this be? Then ask students to learn the history of UFC and apply it to the hot topic they have chosen. The twist enters when you ask students to decide which kind of social media (had it been around in the 1930s, 1970s—just pick a time) would have been the most effective in ending the dominance of UFC in Latin America or in empowering UFC in its quest to maintain power. Have students create a fictional account, complete with posts (images, messages, links, etc.), in the social media platform they think would be most effective for the cause they are representing. (Here you ask students to empathize and role-play.) In a unit or project like this make sure you require students to keep the environment in mind—ask them, How is the banana driving history?

Other commodities can be tied to the students' lunch boxes and to the deeper past. The materiality of commodities works in our favor because they are tangible and can be traced. As we saw with the banana, commodity chains, as economists know them, are logical enough for most students to grasp but not so obvious that students have necessarily thought about them before. If you want to examine two of the earliest traded (and most lucrative) commodities from the Americas, chocolate and tobacco provide surprising and early examples of what Marcy Norton calls "botanical ambassadors" that changed, and were changed by, Europe. Her book *Sacred Gifts, Profane Pleasures* explores the way dried leaves and an odd Indian beverage challenged European customs and enjoy ubiquity today.[7] As a drink, chocolate energized the fatigued and uplifted the depressed long before coffee or tea appeared at the breakfast table. Tobacco was first associated with Indian paganism but quickly grew to be a staple for clergymen and a large source of state revenue. Links to Starbucks's recent reinvention of hot chocolate and to tobacco's medical downfall can be used to build relevance and an analysis of change over time.

Another route is to go with food staples. There are two American plants that became commodities and that work well to center the processes of European dispersal and capitalist consolidation. Maize, or corn, provides a parable for European expansion, and wheat in the Western Hemisphere allows us to reconcile the reach of the market by the early twentieth century.

The late Mexican anthropologist Arturo Warman argued that Mexicans invented corn.[8] This strikes students as a logical fallacy. Corn is a plant. How does someone invent a plant? Very slowly and very intentionally. One can begin the discussion by asking students to do a survey of a grocery store section of processed food. (The cereal aisle or the soda aisle are particularly good for this assignment.) Have students count how many items contain high-fructose corn syrup (or corn syrup of any kind). Once they have that information, I assign articles on how HFCS is manufactured and the public outcry about its ubiquity in foods. How, I ask, did this simple grass become so powerful and omnipresent?

The story begins a long time ago. By showing images of teosintes, the closest heritage land races of modern maize that are hardly different from grasses and contain what would be a cob only slightly larger than a paper-clip, students' interest in the origins of this nutritionally suspect food is piqued. Amerindians consciously manipulated these teosintes until they came up with something close to modern corn. This slow invention, perhaps the world's first feat of genetic engineering, took place somewhere in the southern Mexican highlands.[9] Maize is similar to other major cereal grains (wheat, rice, barley, etc.) in that it offers more calories than it takes in, but it is also different in part because of its reliance upon humans to propagate it, much like the banana. As anyone who has removed the husks from a fresh cob knows, the grains are buried deep inside sheaths, which effectively means the plant cannot get the seeds out to reproduce on its own. Maize came to be cultivated throughout the region, hybridized into different colors, textures, and varieties of sweetness, and began to spread according to human preferences. Over centuries it radiated throughout the Americas, nourishing the Inka in the Andes and greeting the Pilgrims in New England.

After the arrival of Europeans, maize too crossed the Atlantic. As Alfred Crosby has pointed out, maize's reliance on humans, its rapid growth cycle, and its viability in marginal land made it a grain of choice throughout the Old World. Wheat returned five grains for every one sown, while maize generously offered twenty-five. It could be planted nearly every year, reducing fallow time and improving cultivating efficiency. Italy came to depend on polenta, central Europeans baked cornbread, and cornmeal mush became a staple of peasants throughout France.[10] Africans also adopted maize. James McCann's research cogently takes the crop through Africa, where corn became food, fodder, and fuel after being introduced, most likely, by a slaving ship.[11] Here maize is tied to specific political and economic histories as it transitioned from largely a field crop for livestock to a replacement for traditional crops and a source of human sustenance by the late twentieth century. McCann points out some of the societal and health implications of this transition to maize—such as the link between corn and a major malaria epidemic in Ethiopia's highlands—and in doing so provides insight into the many interpretations of the transnational nature of maize.

Maize's ubiquity in the early modern world takes some excavation. In today's modern societies, maize is there for all to see. Or taste. From the hog farms of Iowa to the fuel in our cars and the ingredients in our soft drinks, corn fortifies nearly everything. In some real sense most food is Mexican food.

How does this partial biography of corn help us to highlight the processes of globalization and relevance? Much like the banana, the study of corn centers the frictions of encounter by looking at a single commodity and its history. As Crosby, Warman, and McCann point out, corn was long associated with poverty. It was a fuel that fed the stomachs of the poor, and in this way it was part of the shift in agriculture that subsidized industrialization as a process that remains essential in food production in the twenty-first century. Industrialization drew millions of people away from farming, but these people still needed to be fed. By increasing the yield of agriculture through the introduction of Amerindian crops—not just corn but also potatoes—industrial workers could fill their stomachs. This resulted in a major transformation in Europe, including, as Crosby puts it, "an enormous surge not only of numbers—from 60 million in 1400 to 390 million in 1900—but of economic growth, intellectual achievement, and material power."[12] This is one way corn takes us to capitalism.

Centering this process involves the constant balance of content and conversation. Depending on the course and the goals for global or regional coverage, one can pair readings of Warman or Crosby with questions about the social implications of changing diets. Directed discussions work well here, using visual organizers. For instance, write the word *corn* in a circle in the center of the board with five radiating spokes; then ask students to turn to their neighbor and identify which historical actors are connected to corn. This helps students begin to see the networks and connections that are essential in understanding the global processes in which they eat and live. After a few minutes of brainstorming, students should come back together and write the connections they made on the end of the spokes (peasants, workers, bakers, sailors, etc.). Students can then identify how each group is connected and write these responses on the spokes (through labor, through consumption, through culture, etc.). Discussion will reveal that corn highlights differentials in power. Often the links are abstract and slow moving, although many can be traced back to sixteenth-century European encounters with other parts of the world and the spread and distribution of Amerindian plants alongside European people and animals. Visual organizers and mind maps can help bring processes out of the shadows by showing the ways that people in the world of commodities have been connected through the exchange and use of these commodities, all of which are produced from the earth. As a process, the rise of capitalism involves a reconceptualization of people, plants, and animals into labor, goods, and profits.

For help here we can turn to the industrialization of wheat cultivation in the mid- to late nineteenth century. Sterling Evans has written a wonderful book on the commodification of wheat and twine that can be excerpted or used in totality in a lesson on the relevance of environmental history and its connection to globalization. In *Bound in Twine*, Evans traces the hemispheric connections between wheat and the cultivation of henequen (the raw fiber used to make twine to bind wheat). In the mid-nineteenth century, as U.S. agribusinesses began to intensively mechanize their wheat production through the use of such implements as McCormick's reaper, the impetus to trade the commodity at farther and farther distances intensified. By the beginning of World War I the opportunity to win the war with wheat propelled American wheat farmers into international diplomacy. The reach of wheat supplies necessitated a new way to bind the wheat, as the metal ties used previously were no longer workable for a variety of reasons. Enter henequen, the agave-based fiber native to the Yucatán in Mexico. Mexican farmers and the Mexican government worked together to increase production in order to bring economic development to the generally impoverished (and once believed to be uncultivable) region. Evans paints a picture of plantation-like labor regimes that eventually connected Mexico with the plains farmers in the United States and Canada. This commodity chain had implications for the arid environs of the Yucatán and the short grasslands of the Great Plains, but more importantly this globalization of agave and wheat had profound ramifications for the humans who cultivated them. Increasing capitalization and industrialization of the production of these commodities led to ecological and economic exploitation of land and labor that transcended national and cultural barriers.[13]

It is in the focused study of an ecological network such as the henequen-wheat complex that the relevance and broad applicability of studying environmental history can become most real for your students. There, in their gluten-laden bread and cereals, lies a past that is sometimes inspiring and sometimes disturbing but always relevant. Whether it is corn, bananas, wheat, or some other food, the global and transdisciplinary relevance of environmental history can be taught and learned by a foray into our students' lunch boxes. Taking the first week or so to make this "field trip" will pay big dividends as your students begin to see nature and networks in everything. It will plant an important seed to encourage them to explore the world beyond history and beyond the classroom.

Chapter Two

The Seed

USING LEARNING OBJECTIVES TO BUILD A COURSE

A SEED FACILITATES emergence. Here it provides a metaphor for generating environmental perspectives, questions, and possibilities that are otherwise missing from traditional ways of teaching about the past. The seed also gives us a concept for planning what we want to grow and for making environmental history something we *do* rather than something we *know*.

One place to implicitly and explicitly teach this commitment to skill acquisition is by intentionally embedding higher-order thinking skills into our course design. A critical step is to determine course objectives, or learning outcomes, and tailor the course to them. You can call these whatever works for you; we mean usually four to six clear, attainable, measurable, and specific skills your students will have practiced and hopefully begun to master by the end of the course. We emphasize skills over content to ensure that the methods historians use inhabit an intentional place within a course's structure. Content can always be worked in, but skills too often get underemphasized or left out if they aren't planned for. Determining these at the outset gives you a framework — both linear and recursive — onto which you can hang your big ideas for student learning. Chances are you have these things in mind even if you have not yet communicated them to your students outright. We suggest you take the time to identify course objectives for your clarity of mind, if not theirs. From the first day of class, when we introduce the syllabus, we both emphasize the ability to think critically, historically, and empathetically in our objectives. Effective communication and collaboration, as well as expert evaluation of sources (information literacy) figure prominently as well. These goals likely sound familiar, as they make up the essential facets of the discipline of history, not just its environmental dimensions. Placing skill-based goals in the syllabus and making sure the students know that those will be assessed using a variety of methods can help create a foundation for sustained and deliberate discussions of learning throughout the course.

As a few examples, skill-based objectives could look something like this:

- Students will learn how to ask meaningful questions about the human experience and gather a varied body of evidence to find answers to these questions.
- Students will demonstrate the ability to understand different perspectives to such a degree that they will reason empathetically with historical subjects of differing races, ethnic heritages, classes, cultures, sexualities, and genders.
- Students will become adept and confident at evaluating the veracity and reliability of sources as well as juxtaposing different perspectives to compare and connect a wide variety of times and places.

These might strike you as overly general and as more useful for the instructor than the students. Perhaps. They can be tweaked and refined to apply specifically to the persistent set of issues raised by environmental historians. Take the first objective, about questions and evidence. By introducing the notion of relationships between humans and nature and the idea of evidence as emanating from different types of sources, this can become specific to an environmental course. The objective might then be "Students will learn how to ask meaningful questions *that span various time scales* about the *relationship between humans and nature* and gather a varied body of evidence, *including scientific field guides, newspaper articles, and children's stories*, to find answers to these questions." On the other hand, if you have a more general objective, like those above, for your world or Western civilization courses, fitting the environment into it becomes less daunting.

You might not agree with these outcomes. Maybe you think students should instead learn to write critically and concisely using a book review format. Maybe you emphasize narrative and expect students to organize their thoughts into coherent, logical, and compelling stories based in historical evidence. Maybe you want them to be able to evaluate the persistence of distinct civilizations in specific landscapes or be able to synthesize the ways human-caused changes to the planet have been complex, contested, and yet understandable by using visual or graphic displays of data. That's what makes history so adaptable; you should formulate and articulate your own learning outcomes as part of your plan for your course. We believe that environmental history is, at its core, history. Building a new environmental direction does not have to mean starting from scratch; it can mean simply asking questions driven by the perspective of nonhuman nature to allow students to digest the knowledge and perfect the skills that are present in all good history courses.

Learning outcomes vary within and beyond disciplines, but the features of high-quality design build strategically on each other. You will see examples of this in each chapter of this text. Whether or not you find it useful to rewrite your objectives, include them on your syllabus, or discuss them with students, the larger point here is that identifying your own goals for student learning at the outset makes your choices for content, assignments, and evaluation more focused and transparent. These goals should help to orient you on those bleak October mornings when you ask yourself, Why am I teaching this course this way? What am I trying to accomplish? Learning outcomes should ground your instruction and allow you to build an authentic, meaningful, flexible course. Plant them early, tend them gently, and sprinkle them throughout your daily and weekly plans. They will root your teaching in good practice and support active learning. In other words, use your course objectives as the seeds of learning for your course. The rest of this chapter provides some examples we've used to link our objectives with activities and assignments.

For instance, I start a course in global environmental history with an assignment in which students locate their childhood home on Google Maps. The assignment connects to the second learning outcome, "evaluating different perspectives," because a crucial part of achieving this skill is ensuring students practice identifying their own perspective. It also goes far in enhancing their sense of place (see more in chapter 6). I start the exercise by modeling a tour of my childhood home in the fantastically named suburb El Dorado, on the outskirts of Santa Fe, New Mexico. But I don't start in 1979, when I moved there; instead I digitally walk them through the territories of nearby Pueblo peoples, over some of the nearby hills described for their uses (such as Placer Mountain), and into the geometrically staggered National Forest lands. I point out the absence of chronological depth on the present-day map and how hard it is to tell what names or landscape designations came first or last. Because Google Maps displays transportation routes, I ask the students to think about what the Spanish encountered when they first rode their horses here. Spanish names provide hints—Agua Fria, Los Alamos, and La Ciénega—as we toggle among earth, map, and hybrid views, taking in the differences. Especially striking are the curved subdivision roads and relative greenery within the neighborhood, contrasted with the desert brown beyond. We then trace where the Santa Fe Railroad met up with the Camino Real and consider what would cause a developer to create a suburb relatively far (a twenty-minute drive) from amenities like gas and groceries. Place-names, travel routes, and land uses become clues to the past.

I next give students some class time to digitally tour their own past and look at what resides there now. While many of us transient moderns have several possible homes, students should choose the home they know the best. After taking the time to look, think, and ask, students write a short essay due within the first two weeks of class describing what their home was like when they were a child and then speculate on what was in its place one hundred and one thousand years before them. This is a short exercise; it could be thought of as a formative assessment since it precedes and informs later work, and it is imaginative and creative and designed to be shared. The brief paper requires mainly that students be probative and creative with their questioning (which, of course, is another learning outcome). Students almost instinctively type their address into Google and find interesting historical tidbits—phone books, county titles, even place-name definitions. I also introduce them to the geographic information system (GIS) maps of the General Land Office, which can tell them if (or, more likely where we live, when) their home was part of a homestead plot or a land patent and how it was divided.[1] This allows us to center historical questions: How do you know what was there one hundred years ago? How can you find out? What sorts of evidence would you need? Are there travelers' accounts that help us generalize? Legislative records that address patterns of changing land use? Scientific studies of woodland composition, including charcoal deposits or pollen spores? Is it harder to imagine the land one thousand years ago? Why? At its core this brief exercise is about the ways students can find out what came before. But it is also about method: how they may begin to formulate interesting questions. If the class is sufficiently international to encounter childhoods beyond the United States, more questions arise, often including the most revealing: Why change homes? Depending on their age and level of digital curiosity, students may not have viewed their childhood home from above—that alone gives a new perspective.

The exercise is designed to personalize and ground students in the ways the environment has contributed to their own perspectives on the past. One could just as easily do an assignment that removes the landscape— asking students to trace their family's genealogy, for instance. Better yet, one might ask students to carry out both genealogical histories and place histories and then compare the stories that emerge. In having the actual place be part of the process, students arrive at environmental history questions sooner. This opens up a conversation about perspective and value. If the land where a student grew up was a forest, why was that forest there? Is it still there? Why or why not? This invites students inside the ways environmental history makes connections.

After introducing methods as skills with this exercise, historiography enters the picture. I use excerpts from two books that examine the settling of the Americas in dramatically different ways. William Cronon's *Changes in the Land: Indians, Colonists, and the Ecology of New England* is a classic text in environmental history, and the argument is laid out clearly in the title and the first pages of the text. As one of the most widely read books in the field, it lends itself to an examination of how to go about finding who inhabited your home before you did (in a broad sense). But it is also a strikingly neutral text; Indians and colonists had different ways of using the land, and these amounted to "changes." As Cronon says in the preface, "Different peoples choose different ways of interacting with their surrounding environments, and their choices ramify through not only the human community but the larger ecosystem as well." He goes on to say, "The shift from Indian to European dominance in New England entailed important changes in the ways these peoples organized their lives, but it also involved fundamental reorganizations in the region's plant and animal communities."[2] Changes, differences, and reorganizations are all generalizations students recognize as hard to dispute (indeed I beg them to make more provocative and forceful claims in their own work!), but they provide a great starting point. What people do, and how they do it, changes the world around them. And different people do different things. This forms a basic premise of environmental history—what those changes and differences *mean* is where it starts to get good.

By contrast, I next introduce students to some material from Warren Dean's *With Broadax and Firebrand: The Destruction of the Brazilian Atlantic Forest*. This text describes the particular setting of the Atlantic Forest—once as complex and diverse as the Amazon—and its gradual transformation at the hands of humans. From the formation of the land and growth of the forest to the arrival of human inhabitants and modern drives for development, Dean's focus is on the remarkably nonneutral *de-*

struction of this place. In the first pages of his text Dean describes his view out of an airplane window headed south toward Rio de Janeiro. He notes that "it is a landscape scarred by human striving" and that these "manifestations of civilization" show how "urbanized people took possession here five hundred years ago." He goes on to claim that "Forest History, rightly understood, is everywhere on this planet one of exploitation and destruction," and "the disappearance of a tropical forest is therefore a tragedy vast beyond human knowing and conceiving."[3] Our class can then have a discussion about how language — even a title — reveals important clues about the perspectives that lie within.

This sets up the class for ready attention to the lenses that are used by different scholars and the types of attention afforded to different lands.[4] One can imagine a similar comparison with Ramachandra Guha's *Unquiet Woods*, about India, and Nancy Langston's *Forest Dreams, Forest Nightmares*, about Oregon, or any number of excellent works on forests around the world. What matters is that students begin to identify progressive or declensionist tales from relatively small samples of texts and then circle back to the language in their first essays to probe their own biases. This creates the expectation that identifying perspectives is a fruitful way to understand why people make the decisions they do. In other words, these texts help us plant seeds.

Once the seeds of personal relevance and scholarly perspective are built into a class, it is time to encourage discussions defining some of the terms that environmental historians use. *Nature*, or at least *nonhuman nature*, is among the most problematized of terms. (By contrast, *environment* has hardly been touched.) Raymond Williams argues that *nature* is perhaps the most complex word in the English language. But other terms matter too — descriptive ones such as *change* and *destruction* but also evaluative terms such as *pristine*, *sacred*, and *fragile*. I often make this a time to discuss continents and their boundaries — a discussion I borrow from classes on Latin America and works like Felipe Fernandez-Armesto's *Americas: A Hemispheric History*. Many U.S. students have not considered the term *America* or, better yet, *Americans* as applicable to people from Brazil and

Guatemala. Recognizing that this most common of terms is power-laden gives us an example of how geography is contested and must be contextualized.

I next plant the seed of the neutral scholar. That is, I ask students to refrain from using *we* and *us* to talk about events that happened in the past at which they were not present. I even strategically interrupt students in the first few weeks to get inside their heads about this. I explain that "we" did not bomb Nagasaki, and "we" did not kill the last passenger pigeon. Actual people—or clear categories of people—did these things, and it is the work and obligation of history to say who is responsible. Naming names and pointing fingers is an act of courage and a seed that must be planted to combat the false nationalism that masks real power differentials, inequality, and culpability. Especially as it applies to foreign policy, colonialism, acts of war, and environmental dilemmas, the power of history is holding people accountable for their actions. If everyone in every classroom shares the blame or gets the credit for something in which "we" did not all participate, however passively, then the real actors do not get their due. By calling students out when they speak aloud—and asking them to stop "we, we, we-ing" all over the classroom—I set the tone that their papers should also avoid the passive *we*. I see this both as a seed of inclusivity, that is, a way of bringing in students from underrepresented communities and foreign countries or with distinct identities, and as a seed of specificity in terming perspectives.

These sorts of key words and clues to perspective are important to address early on because they alert students to the relationships between critical reading and evaluative writing. The term *ecosystem* is another one worth examining because it shifts students from thinking about nations to thinking about natures. Although the term itself is historically recent to the past few decades, it helps to describe certain parts of nature, thus providing an alternative to political boundaries. Nature defines an ecosystem—by the border of an island, the banks of a lake, or the extension of a desert—and political delineations may or may not coincide. But nature's lines are rarely stark. How different people use the land they live on is one way to gauge not just their perspectives on the land but what aspects of nature they value. Take the forest, a landscape that to most U.S. Americans today is universally benevolent or at least ambivalent; even if you don't see it as a site for recreation or spiritual rejuvenation it is easily seen as a storehouse for future use. Forests, in Cronon's as well as in Dean's studies, are often large expanses, so they seem primeval because they are much bigger than humans. It is easy to get lost among the trees in a forest because the horizon is obscured, adding to the forest's mystery and power. But forests are not universally valued or valuable. Depending on the scope and geography of your class, you might take New England as one example and the West African savannah as another.

Rather than a landscape lost to the modern world, tree cover in New England today is near its greatest extension in at least two hundred years. The explanation for this is of course historical: the more industrialized this region became, the more farms and pastures reverted back to woods. When people left homesteads where they had to work continuously to keep back the forest, the trees recolonized abandoned lands. People had help — from animals, implements, fires, and more — but much of the colonial conversion of woodlands in this region was soft conversion, which means that once it stopped, forests could (and did) return. For an ecologist, these twenty-first-century forests are quite distinct from their eighteenth-century predecessors in terms of diversity and structure, showing that although cycles recur, history never wholly repeats. An interdisciplinary team of scholars centered at the Harvard Forest have zeroed in on this phenomenon and described its dynamics. This "Wildlands and Woodlands" initiative has generated some terrific teaching maps and documents that summarize what has resurged and where.[5] Students find this counterintuitive: they are used to thinking of the U.S. West as wild and wooded and not the former thirteen colonies. I find this sort of example can do wonders for planting another kind of seed: one of hope. That is, students can learn to see that some — but not all — changes are just changes. Some — but not all — destruction can be reversed. Knowing the difference is part of knowing the past. Allowing them to see how New England can regrow its forests gives a deep perspective on what sorts of ecosystems regenerate because their species are fewer, their diversity lower, and their development slower. And it gives students a keener sense of urgency for those, like Dean's tropical forests, that cannot return on a similar timescale.

Half a world away is another place where the dynamics between forests and pastures have led to persistent—and persistently incorrect—assumptions about land use and peoples. In *Misreading the African Landscape*, James Fairhead and Melissa Leach examine islands of forest amid expanses of savannah that had long been regarded as the last relics of larger forests degraded by overuse.[6] By questioning these assumptions about the past, they show that the islands are in fact the opposite: generative spots created by local uses that turned vegetation more woody. Deforestation has been a clarion call for forest protection, but Fairhead and Leach offer good reasons for us to look at deforestation as more than a simple process of people mistreating the land. This is where ecology matters and environmental perspectives help to unveil critical relationships among people, not just between people and their environments.

Attending to language and building probing questions are ways of *doing* good history. They have a particularly crucial role in a class that, at the outset, claims to give attention to nonhuman actors. Pointing out that these are transferrable skills helps move students away from the often overwhelming amount of content that can exist in a global class. This is not to say that content doesn't matter, but doing environmental history involves the search for novel sources and the consideration of less obvious perspectives within those sources. To attend to this, I make the point to students that discussion is our laboratory; it is not an optional time filler, but instead it allows them to practice and develop their ideas as much as problem sets in mathematics classes or lab experiments in biology. I try to model discussion as a place to plant our seeds of perspective.

Speaking of discussion, repeated roundtables are one pedagogic technique that can be used to discuss a discrete historical topic. I use the term *roundtable* to emphasize the collective character of these discussions and to formalize them. I build three or four into the syllabus as I would readings, papers, and exams. This strategy helps foster preparedness and perspective as skills, and it highlights the ways that history facilitates conversations. During the class session before the scheduled roundtable, I have students sign up for specific roles distributed evenly across the readings so they have a position to read for. The first roundtable matters for setting up the next, and the first is the most binary. I title it "Hunter-gatherers versus Farmers," and it follows up on readings about these modes of life. All students are assigned the same two or three articles that sketch out the pros and cons of either lifestyle, but they are asked to read for their assigned role more carefully. I find Jared Diamond on Mesopotamia and Charles Mann on ancient Peru get to the point quickly and work well in this early debate where engaging material and fodder for dispute are critical.[7] On the day of the roundtable, we move the desks to form a literal roundtable and proceed with a deepening set of questions around the topic. I first ask students to describe the reading most tied to their designated perspective, and then inquire what benefits there were to their assigned way of life. We proceed to discuss what types of labor, social organization, and contingencies are involved. I write the most poignant comments on the board for elaboration. I have students switch roles at the end, and we vote to determine who would rather have been a hunter-gatherer or a farmer. Much to their initial surprise, almost no one chooses farmer!

Endless variations exist to the pedagogy of a roundtable, but I find that building them into the syllabus, assigning students a focus beforehand, and preparing provocative and probative questions makes them get better over time and allows for more perspectives to enter into discussions of environmental issues. Later roundtable topics I've used deal with specific ecosystems (for instance, rivers, where we read articles on the Anacostia River in Washington, D.C., the Yellow River in China, and the damming of rivers in the USSR and the U.S. West), urban environments (Mexico City, Paris, and Curitiba, Brazil), and sometimes a specific form of resource exploitation such as hunting or oil drilling. You might consider how roundtables allow you to fit in content about areas of the world that slip out of your lectures while still ensuring that skills such as identifying perspectives remain central to each day's work. For example, you might ask students: What do forest histories of France tell us that forest histories of Tanzania do not? How did the introduction of cash crops differ in Colombia, Cambodia, and Canada? New and innovative scholarship emerges continually, and roundtables are a low-risk method of integrating recent studies.

Planting seeds allows us to see possibilities. By mixing new and old, fresh sprouts emerge from a richly textured field. With the environment resting at the center, history becomes a series of junctures and choices, not a list of events. People employ different strategies to deal with what they perceive as problems, and the results expose many points of engagement. Ultimately planting a seed is an act of faith. The life that grows out of that seed may not develop precisely as the planter expects, but with repeated and careful attention it will certainly have a number of opportunities open to it.

Chapter Three

The Hatchet

WIELDING CRITIQUE TO RECONSIDER PERIODIZATION AND PLACE

ENVIRONMENTAL HISTORY can be taught without mastering an entirely new field. Reconsidering the basic elements of a history class—time and place—and redefining pivotal transitions can allow you to take different temporalities seriously and make space for the environment. For example, Wendy Petersen-Boring describes the emergence of competing timeframes when she reorganized her history courses using the lens of sustainability.[1] She explains that most students arrive in classrooms with a vague sense of the progression of the human past, at least for Western civilizations. If you ask them, they might suggest this order: prehistoric (cave paintings), Egypt (pyramids), Greeks and Romans (gods and gladiators), Dark Ages (churches and the plague), the Renaissance (paintings), the Enlightenment (science), and modern times (exploration and nation-states). But a different timeline outlines the past according to environmental history. This involves a three-part division based on energy: provisioning (hunting-gathering), planting (agriculture), and producing (industrial), or more basically a shift from energy plucked from the sun to energy pulled up from under the ground. Although the dimensions are vaguely familiar, very few students know this second chronology. Pointing out and interrogating the discrepancy begins a critique: What values are centered in each periodization? Where is nature? Politics? Human ingenuity? Where do the timelines intersect, and where do they diverge? The way we set apart segments of time forms the basic skeleton of a course and reveals our intellectual commitments. By drawing these timelines on the board or having students visually or physically construct them in groups you allow the juxtaposition to tell vastly different stories about the human past. Involving students in this timeline exercise might form the introduction to an environmental history course, but it could just as easily kick off a course in Western civilizations.

It can be rewarding to build environmental history into a course you already know well. The process of reworking classic approaches to the past to include the environment means finding ways to recognize, critique, and uncover points of intersection between human developments and the use of nature, be it energy, food, minerals, climate, or other crucial material. Then you can nestle these insights purposefully into a course. In order to introduce a new subject or free up time and space in your course it is necessary to trim away some traditional stories, methods, and approaches and replace them with insights from environmental history. Using some examples of climate history, this chapter explores periodization and place as techniques for carving out room for nature in your narrative. Borrowing from Paul Robbins, we call this approach a hatchet.

In his introduction to political ecology, a kindred field to environmental history that takes up the ways political, economic, and social factors intersect with environmental issues, Robbins describes political ecology as a hatchet, a way to "expose flaws in dominant approaches to the environment favored by corporate, state, and international authorities, working to demonstrate the undesirable impacts of policies and market conditions, especially from the point of view of local people, marginal groups, and vulnerable populations."[2] To engage this metaphor, environmental history need not have the same political sympathies for the less powerful (although it often does), but the hatchet critique is useful for thinking about strategies for adding environmental history to traditional historical narratives. In the way many courses are taught, the environment is nearly nonexistent; human history might have taken place anywhere. In some courses the environment is backdrop, a lovely bucolic setting onto which humans act out their lives. In others, nature is victim, the brutalized and innocent recipient of harsh abuse or negligence. Employing the hatchet means we expose and then cut away at these falsehoods to grow more complete narratives.

The hatchet is a weapon you can wield as an instructor and curriculum designer in order to carve out space for nature to enter the classroom. If you want to teach energy regimes, some pyramids and churches might have to go. Alternatively they might have to be shown to be the fruit of immense amounts of energy, which required political forces to coalesce. But the hatchet is also a tool, something you can teach your students to use to apply to what they already know and are currently learning. What do we lose if the pyramids are dropped out of the narrative? What if the triumph of science is stained by the pollution of coal? The hatchet, our technique of critique, aims to ask pointed questions about the core structure of a history course—time, place, and the connections between the two. The hatchet can also be generative. By critiquing with pointed and directed questioning, values and choices are revealed and new approaches can begin to grow. This chapter provides ideas for critique as a transformative tool of creation.

Another useful way to insert the environment into the longer and deeper human story, besides energy, is to think about the weather. Adding periodizations offered by past climatic change to the general human narrative provides new junctures and turning points. It is worthwhile to note at the outset that climate history is difficult to master. Climate change as a topic (both in its early form and today) is unwieldy, all-encompassing, and abstract. It is full of abrupt and slow changes, reversals, pulses, equilibriums, and, for our students, many false preconceptions. Not to mention it is largely written by scientists and displayed in charts rather than narratives. If left to geochemists and climatologists, climate might not be connected with the political, economic, and social changes wrought in its path. All the more reason it should find a home in a history class! The lack of certainty and constant contingency of the climate makes for a muddled story of short- and long-term change and consistent variability. But such complexity is the core of great history. From complexity emerge suggestive techniques and temptations for how to plan a course and for how students might approach the past.

Let's take the Medieval Warming as one example. The period from about 900 to 1275 or so, also known as the Medieval Climate Anomaly, had a global coherence because of an enduring climatic pattern that included a warm North, a monsoon surge in Asia, and severe tropical droughts near the Equator.[3] This is a difficult era to characterize globally, but introducing the climatic anomaly provides a lens that helps contextualize the rise and fall of various cultures. For instance, in a history of the Americas class I give a lecture on the Norse and the Maya, two civilizations that students rarely pair in the same thought. During the Medieval Warming, the Vikings extended their travels to Iceland and Greenland and then the shores of North America. Warmer temperatures meant less sea ice, easier traveling, and arable land along the coastal fringes. But for the Maya, the climatic shifts meant drought, which added catastrophic pressures to already overtaxed cities, triggering starvation and ruin. Of course climate was not the only factor influencing Norse and Mayan events, but it is useful and surprising as a comparative thread. Whether through exploration or expansion, societies were shaped by fluctuations in the natural environment. I have thought to expand this lecture in a world history class to include the expansion of Song China or the silent testimony of Chaco Canyon and Angkor Wat so that the larger pattern of transition due to climatic change appears. In other words, a gradually warming climate seemed advantageous for northwestern Europe, but the droughts proved catastrophic for peoples in the American Southwest and the regions of the Yucatán. However configured, the notion of the Medieval Warming helps to bring a diffuse era of ups and downs into a more dramatic story of how climatic change carries alternate fates.

If the Medieval Warming claims new ground for climate in our chronologies, it also opens up space for the Little Ice Age, the subsequent six centuries of cooler and unsettled climate. This time of cooler temperatures and increased precipitation over much of the globe is not well known to most students. A helpful text here is John Richards's *Unending Frontier*, which provides an environmental approach to the early modern world that frames the complex set of issues related to this climatic shift. He asks — and attempts to answer — the question of what effects climate variations have had on human societies. For instance, in Switzerland annual data on wine production show a pronounced slump in the early seventeenth century that correlates with an extended sequence of very cold and wet summers that reduced the output of and sugar in grapes. Consumers reacted by shifting to beer, although rye prices also reflected unfavorable conditions. Some historians have taken this scarcity a step further and linked the dwindling harvests with the increased burning of witches after 1560. Witches were scapegoated for causing thunder or hail storms and blamed for crop failures or diseases.[4] Adding climate to the tale of witch burning enlarges our explanations beyond gender and culture. Exciting new research is suggesting ways that fashion, too, adapted to the cooling trend by featuring heavy drapery and multiple layers, as well as furs.[5]

A single region is hardly enough to understand the Little Ice Age. Comparison helps. In the tropics the idea of an ice age is a misnomer; the more important climatic shift was that of precipitation. Rather than trigger a period of dearth, as experienced in Switzerland, West Africa's more plentiful rainfall (especially in the sixteenth and seventeenth centuries) had profound effects on pastoralists, who could expand across the increased savanna.[6] When the region's climate became drier by 1850, towns like Timbuktu formed the limit of cattle zones. Arab camel nomads advanced where agriculturalists retreated south. Or take the experience of colonial Mexico, where the geographer Georgina Endfield describes how drought and flood were the alternating experiences of climatic shifts in different regions. Litigating water became a primary method of responding to various crises in subsistence exacerbated by climate.[7] New research using descriptions of human sensitivity to inclement weather and paleo-climatological reconstructions of plants and minerals can be measured against models of hydrological conditions and records of land use to demonstrate the ways climate decisively worsened social vulnerabilities.[8] By presenting such contrasting stories to students, we can ask them, How did different peoples experience climate change? What were the results? The echoes into the present day are loud enough for all to hear.

While no historian would believe that events in different societies are replicable or that contexts are inherently the same, it is wise to demonstrate how we can (and should) compare apples and oranges. For instance, we might take up episodes that seem impossibly disparate, such as those chronicled by Alan Mikhail's elegant and brief article that describes a volcano that erupted in Iceland and how people subsequently starved in Ottoman Egypt.[9] How could these events be related? Through the volcano's influence over climate, of course. In June 1783 the Laki volcano in Iceland released so much ash into the atmosphere it led to two years of cold summers and extreme winters in Europe, North America, Central Asia, and beyond. Mikhail uses the unlikely juxtaposition of these two places to examine a specific, small-scale instance of past climate change. Laki's eruption reduced the floods from the Nile and for a few years united these two peripheral places. Egypt and Iceland had little obvious connection, then as now, but by centering a natural event, their pasts intertwine in ways that force us to reconsider what it means to talk about global events and to consider climate change as a lived experience.

Teaching these two climatic periods can break up a progressive narrative of the past. Building in examples of contingency and comparisons of similar environmental dilemmas can be both a methodological and a content-based strategy. One can imagine organizing a course around a set of repeated questions that take reoccurring environmental dilemmas as the core. For instance, starting with a question suggested by Mikhail's "Ottoman Iceland" comparison, you might ask, How have past societies responded to climate change? In the early twentieth-century U.S. West the unsustainable farming practices that were encouraged by the international development of World War I and prolific rain brought radical ruin to the Great Plains from the early 1920s to the late 1930s. The Great Depression looks different when the role of the climate and the political economy of the time are paired. Sure, the Dust Bowl was an agricultural catastrophe, but the cause of it was both cultural *and* environmental. This might lead students to ask, Was the ebb and flow of civilizations the result of climate change or of the societies themselves? Such topics and questions prime students to take climate and geography into account as a factor in the "rise of the West." Students begin to see that warming is a relative phenomenon and climate's influence on human societies is hardly new. Drawing upon conversations among elites, Anya Zilberstein has argued that debates over the human role in causing climate change are far from new products of industrialized societies. What has changed is the interpretation of economic and human impacts on environmental change as a negative rather than positive thing. She contends that in the seventeenth- and eighteenth-century British settler colonies of early America, many people believed population growth and human activity were agents in climate warming—and that this was a very good thing![10] That climate change has different effects on different societies may seem a simple lesson, but when paired with larger chronologies it is a small enough change to allow students to watch it play out. Such introspection allows us to better understand today's dramatically warming world. Climate is one example of how environmental history does not necessarily hijack a class onto an entirely new trajectory. It deepens, enhances, and contextualizes information we already know by adding stories that were ignored a generation ago. The hatchet doesn't have to kill; it can just reorganize and refocus.

If you constructed the timelines we discussed at the outset, it's worth recognizing that timelines are not only graphic tools for students. They can provide valuable planning exercises for stitching environmental events into a set course. Selecting a chronology allows you to sketch out what you expect the end result to look like. You might consider creating a timeline for yourself and placing major events or texts on it. Working backward from today and thinking about landmarks in time while also looking at the semester or quarter calendar gives you space to mark the temporal priorities on which to build the course. It's helpful to put these on the syllabus in sections that support your goals. Environmental history perspectives might change the chronology significantly. For instance, in an introductory world history course, political narratives generally break the course at 1350 or 1500 to showcase the shifts in empires or the connecting of the Americas to Asia, Africa, and Europe. An environmental history course might instead take the concept of revolutions—on its face a political or social theme—and include both the Neolithic and industrial revolutions as key markers of humans altering their use and production of energy. A preoccupation with natural processes takes extra effort, but it allows us to uncover deep and slow-moving dimensions of the past. A timeline from the Pleistocene to the present may be liberating!

If you are inclined to go way back in time, an approach that has been dubbed "Big History" specializes in considering larger processes, starting with the universe and moving on to the solar system, life, human evolution, and then modern times.[11] This framework has its proponents—it certainly considers the environment in every stage—but as an approach it hardly fits the capabilities of most historians or their students and does not ease the constraints under which they teach and learn. While the entire universe's history may be too large, privileging the present can obscure lasting and vivid changes occurring thousands of years earlier. The choice is yours to make deliberately and, in doing so, to show students why chronology matters to the framing of the past.

In most curricula the modern period receives more attention because our current sensibilities shape the idea that industry, technology, and capitalism have marked a distinctive rupture between nature and humanity. A quick glance at most history department course titles tells us that political narratives still dominate. Nation-states overwhelmingly determine our eras, define our borders, and decide the content. Within a course the instructor may or may not give ample attention to politicians or policies, but the structural reality of many curricula means that most of us cannot completely abandon political narratives. Some may be reluctant to delve into environmental history because it might unhitch the past and leave society without solid national events and stories around which students can tie changing ideas. Both characterizations are incomplete: it is not that traditional history considers only human ideas and environmental history inserts only natural processes. Both narratives can be subverted strategically with our hatchet.

Here we might take traditional eras on a timeline of U.S. history and overlay them with distinct ideas Americans placed on the natural world. Most classic timelines break at critical wars—the Revolutionary War, the Civil War, the world wars—and between them have westward expansion, Reconstruction and the Progressive Era, and cold war economic expansion. Onto this chronology, where might we put Americans' understandings of nature? We might overlay the energy narrative and the transition to fossil fuels as it industrialized the Northeast and lagged in the South. This could include how automobiles transformed cities and reoriented public life. But another timeline might add the layer of ideology and imagining. For instance, Jedidiah Purdy has described the evolving orientation of Americans' understandings of their place in nature by naming four overlapping phases.[12] The oldest and most dominant, providential republicanism, imagines the natural world as a place for productive use made mostly through private ownership. The second attitude, progressive management, dictates that natural systems will serve human ends only with expert governance over systems such as irrigation, forests, and wildlife. The third view, romantic epiphany, imagines qualities of the natural world echoed in qualities of human experience (such as sublime aesthetics' use as a correction to a pervasively managed world). The fourth understanding of nature, ecological interdependence, is the most recent; it blends aesthetic and ethical attitudes that view human life as continuous with natural phenomena. What happens when we place the traditional and Purdy's ideological timelines against each other? A fierce back and forth emerges without clean breaks and events. All good history courses pay attention to time through snapshots and causal chains, but setting out overlapping points and narrative intersections builds curricular space for nature and how we think about it.

As you contemplate reworking your chronology, it is also worth considering natural disasters as transitional moments, and not just wars or presidencies. Many students today lived through Hurricane Katrina and might be able to reflect on the changes that event brought to New Orleans. They may recall refugees appearing in Houston and St. Louis and the stark images of distress, disillusionment, and despair playing out on television. They likely heard about the breaching of the levies, the incredible fact that New Orleans resides below the river level, or the long-term destruction of wetland habitat that, given different planning and choices, may have buffered the storm so that the Ninth Ward didn't have to. At some future juncture it may become clear this was a turning point in George W. Bush's presidency, but the disaster itself has a history both before and after that hurricane.

Even within the political survey of U.S. history we can carve space for a reimagining of the traditional narrative through a close study of disasters. The New Deal, and specifically John Collier's Indian New Deal, becomes richer in the able hands of Marsha Weisiger as she examines the sheep-reduction strategies of the federal government on Diné (Navajo) lands. Weisiger's work shifts our understanding of a fairly well-known moment in American political history away from a singular focus on Washington bureaucrats toward the more complicated story of environmental (in)justice as it played out in the context of Diné understandings of herding. These understandings were not just ecological or economic, as previous histories have suggested. Rather they were situated in the Diné matrilineal culture and thus profoundly gendered, a nuance that was lost on the Roosevelt bureaucrats who sought simple causes and simple solutions to the problems of overgrazing. While the causes of the ecological disaster on the reservation were multiple, the understandings of those causes differed based on the worldviews of the two parties involved. Here an examination of public policy during times of disaster can be made richer by studying the disconnects between two cultures and among locals and extralocals. These disconnects had very real ramifications for the handling of the disaster, and the misunderstandings of the past continued well into the future. In class this environmental, gendered, and political reexamination of what can seem like a rather dry topic, the New Deal, can be made enthralling for students by using primary sources from the parties involved and asking students to come up with solutions to the disaster based on the information they have before them. This topic and lesson can help ensure students have the opportunity to practice problem solving with empathy, an increasingly important skill in twenty-first-century policymaking. And if you don't have the time or the best classroom setting for such a lesson, then at least exposing students to histories of missed opportunities in dealing with disasters, like Weisiger's, will help them construct links between nature and culture and how different actors in different times think about them both.[13]

Disasters have played formative roles before and beyond the U.S. borders. Historians Sherry Johnson and Louis Pérez have described how hurricanes marked transitions in Caribbean and Atlantic world history.[14] Historians easily recognize the Age of Revolutions from the 1760s to the 1820s, but Johnson inserts the notion of environmental crisis — especially droughts and hurricanes — into the trade policies of the Spanish Empire to produce a more complete accounting of how extreme weather patterns shaped this critical period. Pérez's insights add the nineteenth century, when three successive hurricanes, in 1842, 1844, and 1846, transformed land tenure forms and development strategies on the island of Cuba. Prior to these storms, coffee estates were less expensive to establish, had more modest labor requirements, and held greater opportunities for complementary crops than did sugar estates. One might contend that expanding the coffee estates would have fostered more democratic arrangements but the material devastation of the storms caused coffee growers to contract and sugar estates to expand. Alongside this shift slavery deepened, as did Cuba's dependence on U.S. markets, while commercial export agriculture displaced a more diversified domestic subsistence economy. Certainly the hurricanes did not directly prolong slavery or Cuban dependence, but the storms helped convince landowners to shift crops, which resulted in both. Pérez shows how we might consider foregrounding natural disasters as turning points in economic and even political decisions. Doing so will change the way those events are interpreted.

Defining the place or places for your course provides another way to employ the hatchet. For many historians, locating a course within your geographic field of training is an excellent way of grounding it in a familiar locale. The hatchet encourages you to cut that place into a new form. For instance, a Western civilizations course reinvigorated to add environmental history might include more about European colonies. It was explicitly these foreign environments that gave colonial administrators a new look at their worlds. Richard Grove's claim that "the seeds of modern conservationism developed as an integral part of the European encounter with the tropics" suggests that ideas about nature's destruction were formed not solely in the core but also on the periphery.[15] In the Western Hemisphere, resisting the convention of dividing the Americas in two can highlight natural rather than national phenomena. Courses on North American environmental history do not presuppose the creation of the United States from awkward artificial boundaries. By including Canada and Mexico this framework pushes beyond the nation-state as the only site for historical narratives, building this critique into course design. Oceanic histories similarly challenge how we frame the environment as a site of human culture. An Atlantic or Pacific world framework appeals to some for its political sweep, but it can actually address the history of an ocean as more than a conduit for trade.[16]

Selecting the site involves determining the linking threads that weave the time and place into a coherent story. An environmental perspective offers creative ways of conceptualizing a course. John McNeill frames his history of the twentieth century using spheres, that is, layers of the earth: the biosphere, hydrosphere, atmosphere, and lithosphere (Earth's crust).[17] Biomes, or ecocultural units, such as the Arctic or the Mediterranean could tie time and place together into an organized theme based on the environment, thus exposing novel questions and new answers. A course on the history of the Amazon might be structured to examine the periodic waves of human expansion and retraction that have coursed through the forest. From debates over the extent of agriculture to European exploration and commodity extractions such as rubber, centering the tropical landscape rather than the nine nation-states that share it trims away the binary of colonizer and colonized and opens up opportunities to address the mobility of peoples and the many ways they have built communities in this place over time.

Before becoming overwhelmed with the breadth of possibilities for teaching environmental history, it is useful to reflect on the structures that are already in place. Then wield your hatchet thoughtfully while considering the time and place appropriate for you. Be firm in deciding your parameters and make them explicit in your syllabus — in the introductory paragraph or by sectioning off certain parts of your calendar. Involving students in a discussion of this process can help them envision the deep questions of time and place. Centering comparisons — especially unlikely ones — can be an efficient way of using the newfound space in your course.

Chapter Four

The Llama

RECRUITING ANIMALS TO BLEND NATURE AND CULTURE

THE LLAMA IS AN exotic animal that is nevertheless familiar to most U.S. students. The long-necked, doe-eyed, and wool-covered relative of camels can be commonly found on alpine ranches, in petting zoos, and around multicultural carnivals across the United States. Its appearance invokes the rich Andean cultures of South America that revered the animal as spiritually important and practically useful, and yet the llama's ubiquity raises fascinating questions about the changing and complex relationships among cultures. In other words, the animal has a history.

Humans have generally found hoofed mammals suitable to domesticate and utilize for food, labor, sport, and companionship, but compared to other continents, South America had few large species. About six thousand years ago the first indications of llama and alpaca domestication enter archaeological records, providing evidence of many uses, including consumption of meat, hide, and fiber products, burning of dung for fuel, and manipulation of bones for tools. Unlike large domesticated mammals of Eurasia and Africa, however, these camelids were not milked by people. Andeans consciously resisted using the llama in this way despite the absence of similar species to milk (no cows, goats, or yaks).[1] Given the few available options for gathering animal protein on a regular basis without killing an animal, this seems strange. At least it seems strange until you consider how unusual it is to drink another animal's milk. Llamas do not produce milk in the same volume as cows or goats, but those animals have been bred for their milk for generations, therefore increasing the supply. It seems llamas might have evolved in the same way given human intervention. Why, then, did Andeans ignore llama milk as a protein supplement and source of sustenance? Although this is largely an unanswerable question, it seems most likely that indigenous Andeans had the capacity to milk llamas; they simply lacked the cultural will. The unmilking of llamas — both a factual and a counterfactual claim — raises one example of how animals expose ways of teaching the complicated interface between nature and culture.

Environmental history examines the relationships between human and nonhuman nature, and animals nest precisely in that juncture.[2] Explicit attention to animals allows students to go beyond black-and-white interpretations of the past and venture across species lines, exploring difference and sameness without reinforcing classic binaries. When animals are put at the center of a course or a unit, students begin to examine the ways humans have attempted, to varying degrees of success, to cordon themselves off from other species. Animals — especially the soft, furry, charismatic kind — conjure up human emotions in ways unlike blades of grass or tectonic movements. Because of this, they are an easy sell for environmental history students and a near limitless source of complexity.

From sheep to wolves, animals as subjects of scholarly inquiry have earned book-length treatment from historians.[3] One might be tempted to see this as an extension of commodity studies or perennially popular "food and drink" scholarship, yet there is something captivating about the liveliness of these subjects that bends our moral refractions and broadens environmental historiography. Other scholars have called these new studies an "animal turn."[4] Harriet Ritvo, a leading environmental historian of animals, has pointed out that the study of animals has become more popular, but it remains on the border between disciplines, which is part of the appeal.[5] Precisely because of their almost-but-not-quite humanity, animals provide a seductive rather than reductive approach to the past.

Animals in history deliver both a technique — a way of blending the binaries that may be unwittingly reinforced by human history's "us versus them" construction — and a topic. This chapter roughly sketches a global history course on animals by chronicling overlapping relationships that animals help us to see, profiling animals that highlight those relationships, and explaining assignments designed to allow students to demonstrate their mastery of historical — rather than biological, agricultural, or psychological — approaches to understanding animals. Throughout the chapter I try to point out the comparative and provocative potential animals provide while still grounding the course in the discipline of history and honing historical skills. Unlike other chapters, this chapter discusses the main components of a single course. Do not let this limit you from poaching a unit or assignment and adapting it to your own needs if you do not yet have the curricular space for a history course on nonhumans.

In my Animals in History course I begin with a single core question: How have animals shaped the human past? I explain that we will seek out a variety of different perspectives that may allow us to answer this. Animals provide one of the few topics that can be approached without a strict chronology, so core issues substitute for a traditional timeline. I frame these historical issues as "relationships" to guide the course: extinction and invasion, modes of interaction (adoption, predation, husbandry, symbolism, etc.), and nature and culture. As we work through these relationships, animal profiles give depth with individual examples. Some historians might bristle at the asynchronous organization as a slide into environmental studies or an absence of historical time. Fair enough. Yet I've found that jumping around allows us to engage more deeply with varied, nonhuman timescales. These timescales are competing, overlapping, and contradictory and thus revelatory of environmental processes. The course goes roughly from ancient times to the present, and we construct timelines on everything from the history of zoos to the life cycle of grizzly bears. In traditional time blocks of ancient, medieval, or modern, such scales would be lost or underemphasized. Instead part of the point of the class is to expand what students think of when they think of history.

Such a potentially disorienting journey requires many signposts. To provide these, I set out segments of my syllabus with relationships (extinction and invasion, modes of interaction, and nature and culture) and continually reference them throughout the course. For example, we initially probe issues of extinction and invasion by reading scientific articles and science writers. Science provides one lens through which to consider attempts by various human societies to construct some species as valuable and others as disposable. We then move to the issue of interaction, including the production and consumption of animal-based goods. Here we rely almost entirely on historical studies and chapters to think about how people have turned animals into products, harvested their by-products, or otherwise directly transformed animals for human use. The third set of relationships is the classic nature and culture. To explore this we use specific artifacts (mainly popular images, such as Smokey Bear) and analyze the metaphors they invoke. These three are by no means the only possible sets of relationships that characterize human-animal relations, but they allow us to cover a lot of ground, emphasizing early times and diverse societies. We finish the course with a quick sampling of interdisciplinary theory and student research presentations. The assignments reinforce the historical skills that I prioritize, and by centering historical methodology and reading many examples of historical studies I make this class, at its core, a history course despite the purported emphasis on nonhuman subjects. Such a course is also adaptable to the growing number of formats found outside a regular history curriculum, such as a first-year seminar or an intensive interdisciplinary inquiry course.

Although I don't adhere to a strict chronological narrative, I do like to start the class in the Pleistocene. A quick clip from the 2002 animated film *Ice Age* paired with Paul Martin's classic article "Pleistocene Overkill" leads to a discussion of the relationship between early humans and large animals and sets up the idea of human-caused extinction. Martin argues that in the Americas by the Late Pleistocene (roughly thirteen thousand years ago) populations of mammals exceeding one hundred pounds declined by roughly 70 percent, while smaller species survived. The Americas were already relatively depauperate in large mammals compared to African and Eurasian continents (recall the unmilked llama), and these extinctions further depleted wildlife. Where did all the animals go? Did hunters kill them, or was it another factor, such as climate change or disease? In other words, were the animals subject to overkill, overchill, or overill? To broaden the debates, students also read a more recent scientific article (Martin's is, after all, nearly fifty years old) that surveys current research on human arrival and megafaunal extinction.[6] This controversy raises the issue of extinction as part of the relationship humans have had with other animals for quite a long time. It also provides a platform to discuss current plans for "rewilding" North America with large species, a matter of much scientific and popular interest.[7] We then read the science writers Elizabeth Kolbert and David Quammen to think about more recent extinctions in a roundtable discussion.[8]

The idea of invasion comes next as we begin to examine both intentional and unintentional introductions of species around the world. Reading selections of Alfred Crosby's *Columbian Exchange* gets us grounded, and 1492 becomes a landmark in time for rearranging the world menagerie.[9] The multiplication of pigs, cattle, and horses in the New World greatly rewarded Spanish and Portuguese settlers by provisioning them with readily available sources of protein and beasts of burden. But not all introductions were so purposeful; Crosby points out the Old World black rat hitched a ride across the Atlantic and became the scourge of the Bermudas. We take Crosby's framework of exchange, critique it, and apply it to Australia in the twentieth century.

Using the exquisite forty-five-minute film *Cane Toads* we learn through interviews with people involved that the toad was purposefully introduced to northern Queensland Australia in 1935 to control sugarcane beetles and grubs. The toads spread and reproduced rapidly, and their introduction brought many unintended consequences. People profiled in the film speak in their own words about their own views, from adoration to loathing. The toads are themselves actors in the film, and the jokes, innuendos, and jiggy music make an obscure topic ripe for a discussion of what it means to try to use one animal to control another. Other examples of purposefully and accidentally introduced animals abound: European starlings, snakes on Guam, Brazilian fire ants, Africanized bees, and so on. These cases allow us to discuss by extension social issues of race, immigration, perception, usefulness, and power.

Camels, and of course their brethren the llama, can be a useful way of complicating the idea of invasion as inherently bad or even inevitable and also linking global evolutionary phenomena with the development of diverse societies. On an evolutionary scale, camels in the Arab world, where most students think of them as residing, are recent transplants. Camels spent millions of years in North America, and today Australia boasts the highest wild population.[10] How can this be? Ritvo provides one glimpse by contrasting experiments with introducing camels in the United States and Australia during the modern era. Camels were brought to the United States in the 1850s by the U.S. Army as an alternative mode of transport for patrolling the newly annexed Mexican frontier. A combination of social and environmental factors (for example, the outbreak of the Civil War and the proliferation of spiny cacti that damaged the soft interior of camels' hooves) resulted in a failed invasion despite the fact that the camels were left to become feral. The last sighting of these animals in the desert was in the 1940s. But Australia had the inverse experience. Also introduced in the mid-nineteenth century, camels in Australia came to be used for ordinary commercial purposes, such as carrying materials and delivering telegraphs. By the 1920s camels had suffered replacement by cars and trucks and became superfluous, with many simply abandoned to roam free. The animals multiplied to over one million in subsequent decades, creating the largest herd of wild camels in the world. Since the 1980s the population has been subjected to repeated culls with little effect.[11] Is this parallel introduction a history of human contrast? Environmental determination? Evolutionary serendipity? It can be each of these and more.

Extinction and invasion provide a relational framework — and a notably deep one — for examining human encounters with animals in a global context. The next section I originally conceived of as "Production and Consumption," but I have reworked it as "Modes of Interaction" for reasons described below. A critical lens that enters the course here comes from Marcy Norton's article, which examines birds in early modern Europe and the Americas.[12] She begins with a description of a hawk used in falconry and a chicken used as poultry to characterize European modes of relating to birds, commonly called hunting and husbandry. Her next two examples indicate modes of interaction from the Americas. In an example of a mode she terms predation, eagle feathers were utilized in ritual ornamentation to transfer ferocity; as an example of adoption, baby parrots were brought into families as kin. Norton then traces exchanges, such as the claim that the adoption of baby birds may have been an origin of modern pet keeping, a phenomenon not explainable through either hunting or husbandry. Norton deepens and shifts our Crosbyian ideas of exchange by providing another, more sophisticated and radical set of tools for understanding how people related to and thought about animals: modes of interaction. By comparing how people in the Caribbean and Mesoamerica interacted with birds to the ways people in Europe did, Norton not only excavates a "microhistory of avian-human relationships" but enlivens the entanglements of early modern cultures. Be wary, hers is a difficult article and one that students resist, but it is well worth your effort as an instructor to spend the time, walk them through it, and make sure students understand the incredible intellectual work Norton has done for them. Although we read it in week 6, well into the course, this article enhances the concepts we've already discussed, such as anthropomorphizing animals, and it provides terms that are readily useful and applicable elsewhere. We next look to the sea to understand ways humans have interacted with whales, walruses, and fur seals.[13]

The pliability of "modes of interaction" helps students give depth to relationships such as hunting and domestication but also to thoughtfully consider why specific animals have been targeted for massacre (such as cats in medieval France and donkeys in late twentieth-century South Africa) or even how insects have been mobilized in times of war.[14] Modes of interaction as an organizing concept, more so than the somewhat presentist and structurally limited "production and consumption," allows the consideration of historical sentiments from an early modern era of openness and negotiation intrinsic to encounter. We use this to reconsider what students find familiar in the modern era. If the notion of Pleistocene overkill allows the ancient actions of humans to echo in modern times, Norton's "modes of interaction" gives specificity to the range of possible relationships people have forged with other organisms in past places and times.

The third conceptual pairing built into the course's design — nature and culture — has to do with how people have thought about and represented (rather than simply used) animals in different times and places. This gets to the issue of individual animals as receptacles for particular assumptions. Moreover this unit shows how animals provide ways of talking about certain groups of people. Lauren Derby's analysis of goats and Rafael Trujillo, the dictator of the Dominican Republic in 1930–61, demonstrates this well.[15] Derby argues that the association of the goat with the politician and the emergence of political satire around the goat were an overt parading of his masculinity as well as subversive ways of challenging his power. Certainly more examples from other parts of the world exist of politicians associated with particular animals. One can imagine a comparison here among African or Asian heads of state and symbolic national animals.

Many animals appear linked to children. Long the symbol of fire suppression in the U.S. West, Smokey Bear shows the malleability of even celebrity animals. I have students first read the original children's story by Jane Werner from 1955 and the official description from the Forest Service website.[16] Next we change contexts. Jake Kosek explains through a series of evocative images that this seemingly benevolent bear symbolized "a white racist pig" and "despotic land thief" to Native American, Hispano, and Chicano residents of northern New Mexico who distrusted public land claims and representations of federal authority.[17] James Lewis's short essay, "Smokey Bear in Vietnam," analyzes the altered use of the bear's image during defoliation operations in the Vietnam War.[18] Modified to read "Only *you* can prevent a forest" (rather than "a forest fire"), this "drafting" of Smokey for the war broadened the overseas scope of the

U.S. Forest Service. Examples of contested meanings from other regions and species abound. For instance, it is not coincidental that the notion of animal pedigree emerged in Britain around the same time as genealogical records of elite human ancestry. An affinity for stud books for animals and the Westminster Kennel Club Dog Show are overt displays of figurative kinship and good breeding.

And then there is *Dumbo*. A short clip from this 1941 Disney film allows us to probe the individual and collective identities of species. Elephants open up an investigation of nature and culture using "charismatic megafauna" on a multinational level. In part to build on conversations we've had about the British and Ottoman empires, I use George Orwell's essay exposing the raw violence of an elephant encounter in India, "Shooting an Elephant," in conjunction with Gregg Mitman's article "Pachyderm Possibilities," which examines the changing strategies of scientific research in sub-Saharan Africa. One could easily add selections from Mark Elvin's *Retreat of the Elephants*, a study of China, or one of many excellent critiques of elephants in circuses.[19]

Nature and culture blend with the discussion of artifacts and metaphors for animals (and people). Every few weeks I introduce a series of specific animal profiles to encourage students to see animals first and humans second. These are case studies that allow an in-depth and nicely narrowed focus. I combine some formal lecture with discussions of readings they've prepared. Then we set out to explore visual artifacts and representations and, often, to apply them to an authentic and contemporary issue. Sometimes this includes a geographical switch. For instance, we look first at the nineteenth-century eradication of wolves in Japan and then the near eradication and reintroduction of wolves in the United States.[20] I select animals with provocative pasts and unusual stories—often as ways of getting students to think about societies that are different from their own. There are far too many animals with interesting pasts that could be profiled; I try to emphasize those that have long relationships with humans over time.

The red deer (*Cervus elaphus*), among the most widespread wild herbivores in Europe, provides a good example.[21] By reading a succinct scientific review of the animal's present status, students glean a lot of useful information. Much like elk in North America, throughout their range red deer have been a highly valued game species for millennia and subject to intensive management for centuries. Red deer were featured in some of the world's first conservation areas and today are more populous than they have been in centuries, in part due to a decline in their natural predators but also because of extreme acts of management, including the provisioning of winter fodder. Complicating matters is the fact that red deer have also been recently domesticated; over ten thousand deer farms operate in Europe. Such contradictions raise provocative questions: Are wild red deer in fact wild? What, then, distinguishes a wild or domestic species for reasons of conservation? Who decides, and what does it mean for the red deer?

In order to deepen this profile from information and discussion, I create an application. In this case I say that I'm a philanthropist who would like to spend $10 million on the red deer. I break students up into groups of three or four and give them this charge: they've been hired to provide a simple and compelling case for what can and should be done for the red deer in Europe. They are given forty-five in-class minutes to discuss, research, and put a single PowerPoint slide together, and then each group gets two minutes to present to the class. Because they've done the reading they have some background, but then they furiously research what they can in class and make a pitch. This condensed, on-the-spot, rapid-fire research builds on skills they've been honing all semester, and the exercise's compelling authenticity makes it a more useful class period than a lecture in which I describe challenges facing the animal and the complex ways people in different but adjacent countries interact with wild animals. If red deer don't interest you, consider wild horses, sharks, or pangolins, or start with a part of the world you want to give more attention to and find an animal from there.

Animals add to our classes just as they add to our lives. They evoke our emotions, although never evenly or predictably. They add comic relief, and they awaken students who may be slightly misanthropic. It is tempting to make a class on animals a long version of show and tell, but sadly this doesn't hone critical historical skills. In light of this, however, I employ more creative assignments in this course, playing on the inherent interdisciplinary nature of animal research. In total, students complete four written assignments. The first and most traditional is what I call simply the Long Assignment. I ask students on the first day of class to tell me what their favorite animal is. I write every response on the board, with special emphasis on original answers. I go first and model novelty by offering up the vicuña, a softer, smaller, and wild relative of the llama that appears on the national seal of Peru and nearly went extinct during the mid-twentieth century because its wool is finer and more expensive than cashmere. Building in part on this list, students select an animal; they will be wedded to this animal for the remainder of the semester, culminating in a *cultural* history of the animal in three thousand to four thousand words. Students can choose an individual, even fictional animal, such as Winnie the Pooh, or an entire species, such as the black bear. I discourage selecting something too personal, such as their childhood gerbil, although presidential dogs could be a great topic. The expectations are not much more defined than this, although the techniques from the next three assignments are expected to be integrated into the Long Assignment.

What is meant by cultural history becomes a topic of discussion early on, especially how and if it might differ from social, political, or economic history. How much biology, natural history, and description belong in such a history also gets modeled and discussed as we look at different animal profiles in class. Students work through how one determines a chronological scope for an animal's past, the relative importance of the human society that shares territory with the animal, and the specific factors that change over time in this animal's lifespan. The Long Assignment is due on the final day of class, when we have a Zookeepers' Feast — a modified version of a discussion roundtable where students bring in an image of their animal, sit in a circle, and respond to my interrogation about their animals.

The Long Assignment develops historical skills because it is a work in progress with specific milestones. It is a research paper, but with a twist that makes it seem less daunting. As in most historical research, sources for animal history are a challenge (whether it is one of dearth or abundance), but not an insurmountable one. While it is true that there is no way to go straight to the source and get a buffalo's opinion on the railroad, this lacuna does raise the possibility of juxtaposing other points of view and thinking creatively about evidence. This is where the ancillary assignments come in.

The first support assignment is called the Three Lenses Approach. Shortly after committing to an animal and as a way of ensuring that the students did a bit of digging to confirm they will have enough historical sources, I ask students to read three specific kinds of sources, which we call "lenses." These rotate, but usually I ask students to find a scientific paper (one with a specified date, usually before 1970), a children's story (the date range is open, but older is better), and a series of newspaper articles (say, five articles at twenty-year intervals). These specific demands teach students that databases and search engines are powerful tools for historians and also force them to look at how the treatment of animals may change over time. This is the minimum source base: of course they can supplement. The paper has a strict structure. The first paragraph explains the animal, the human society around it, and the time frame. The next three paragraphs describe the view of the animal put forth by each lens. The point is to come up with an original argument about that animal based on a close and careful reading of these specific kinds of sources. Although the format is somewhat contrived and restrictive, the idea is to narrow in on selecting evidence, critical reading, and organized writing. It is designed—with three lenses—to push students beyond binaries to points that will form part of the ongoing discussion in class. The main criterion is that students make an *interesting* and *nontrivial claim*, that is, one that requires evidence and argumentation, about a specific animal using at least the three types of sources.

The second support assignment is an Animal Policy Brief that comes out of our discussion of modes of interaction. This assignment asks students to identify how an aspect of policy has transformed the life of an animal.[22] Students choose a policy (broadly defined as an action taken by a government body) and explain how it has changed the life of a species.

I make sure we do policy work leading up to this, including looking at the Idaho Fish and Game Hunting License Application, the U.S. Army's policy on service animals, and Japanese policies on whaling, to name a few. In this course section we've discussed butcher's shops in urban spaces and the use of elephants in Ottoman pageantry. We've even considered the moral controversies around cloning Dolly the sheep and the Food and Drug Administration's approval of genetically modified salmon for consumption (without labeling) in the United States. About a week before the assignment is due, we hold a policy workshop, where students bring in the policies they've found that apply to their animals and work in groups using a template of questions analyzing the policy.

For the individual assignment, students select, describe, and analyze a policy critical to their animal, and they must provide a copy of the policy when they turn in their brief. The brief is a summary recommendation to a specific government entity of what it should do about an animal-related issue. It is a formal, practical, applied style of writing intended to demonstrate the ways historical knowledge can inform policy. Because it can be very difficult for students to identify a policy, sending their research into a tailspin, I have considered amending this assignment by providing them with a few common policies from which all students can then draw for their animals (for instance, Idaho's 1874 game laws, the 1916 Migratory Bird Treaty, and the Convention on International Trade in Endangered Species of 1973). In the end the lesson frequently emerges that while individual people use animals, larger forces shape patterns of survival in dramatic ways.

Last comes the lighter side. With the Creature Chronicle, students take a chronological and creative approach by selecting a major world event — whatever that might mean to them — and imagining that event through the eyes of an animal. They are asked to spend four to five pages chronicling the event from the perspective of any animal that logically might have been there. How did alligators view the extinction of dinosaurs? What did Hannibal's elephants see when they crossed the Alps into Italy in 281 BCE? What did Albert, the first monkey launched toward space in 1948, think of his short trip? How did Fuleco, the armadillo mascot of the 2014 World Cup in Brazil, experience the games? On first glance this goes against much of the primary research the first exercise emphasizes, by pushing students to find secondary sources and read against the grain for the silences of the past. To this end the paper must include a bibliography containing three books and four scholarly articles dealing with the event, though not necessarily with the profiled animal. Rather than requiring evidence and argumentation, this assignment asks for students' creative extrapolation and the counterfactual deployment of the possible. The essay can be written in the first person. It's the most flexible and the most polarizing assignment, as some students find it very difficult to compose what amounts to historical fiction, while others object to the Dr. Doolittle–esque mindreading.

We debrief the challenges and benefits of each assignment on the day they turn it in, which contributes to the way they put together their own process of history-making. The scaffolded assignments on animals, and the ways of thinking built into this course, should wiggle their way into students' own habits of mind.

The last set of readings and discussions in the class are theory. This is the inverse of how I teach surveys of Latin America. In those, an early introduction to modernization theory, Iberian culture theory, and dependency theory critically shapes how students come to understand foreign policy, revolution, and development strategies. Front-loading theory gives students a semester to grapple with it. I believe the reverse is true for teaching with animals; concluding with theory gives them a new set of ideas grounded in the historical practices we developed over the semester. Part of the reason for this is that there is not a set of agreed upon approaches to animals or clear theories that fully engage the remit of such a topic. Another major justification for saving theory and ethics to the end is to allow students to form their own ideas about the place of animals in the past. Concluding with selections from Peter Singer's *Animal Liberation* or Temple Grandin's "Thinking the Way Animals Do" allows students to have a semester's worth of examples to bring to the table. Theory and ethics form our penultimate class, with the final day reserved for our "Zookeepers' Feast." This is both lighthearted and serious. We consider which of the animals might devour each other, but we also debate which face the largest challenges in our rapidly humanizing world.

The technique of using animals to blend binaries and center other species has suggested ways you might teach with a llama (or an elephant or a deer...). I'm not advocating that you bring a live llama to class (although they are getting more attention as therapy animals) but that you consider the various ways people have used animals in different societies and what that means for the past and future of human and nonhuman beings.

PART II

Pathways

PART I OUTLINED and explained tools for creating the architecture necessary to build a course. We discussed methods of reaching students on their own terms and assignments that meet clear goals for the acquisition of historical skills. Part II elaborates on this beginning with specific and discrete topics that make sense in environmental history classrooms: understanding science, making sense of place, and harnessing energy. We offer this discussion as a set of pathways or strategies for making connections among the components of a class. Each pathway offers an intellectual justification for how the topic fits into an environmental history class and a set of examples for how the topic might be animated through deliberate and carefully planned instruction. We offer these chapters as part of our ongoing dialogue on how the past can enthusiastically remain present for our students.

Chapter Five

The Fields

SCIENCE AND GOING OUTSIDE

WHEN THE Versicolored Barbet (*Eubucco versicolor*) crashed into the window above our breakfast table, I knew it was not going to be an ordinary meal. He was a spectacular bird with a bold red face, a green crown, blue cheeks, and an electric-yellow chest. Although he lay forever still, the Barbet's dark eyes, feet, and beak accentuated his wildness and impudence. Over Nescafé and eggs, students on this month-long field course took turns observing these intricate details of our feathered friend. Since they'd spent the past two days identifying distant birds in faraway trees, this unexpected death opened a new set of questions about our surroundings and about the past treatment of avian mortality. What happens to scientific specimens? Where do they go? Who stores them? What does it mean to own that knowledge? What is the difference between a dead bird in a museum and a live one in a zoo or a national park? Is death-by-window equivalent to hunting birds to sell the feathers for hats? Are birds a necessity or a luxury to protect?

As this brief experience illustrates, going into the field narrows the gap between environmental history and many of its kindred scientific disciplines, especially natural field sciences. There are many reasons to take environmental history outside. Field courses go beyond traditional classroom walls and into places where history and nature come alive. This can be fun, memorable, and exciting. When planned well, such courses merge experiential learning and applied disciplinary objectives with the personal growth that traveling stimulates. Summer, January term, intensive semester learning experiences, and other immersive arrangements beg for environmental history field courses. Even if you cannot dedicate an entire course to the field, project-based expeditions or even short exercises out of doors can change the context of a course.

Another way to think about going into the field is to consider going into another discipline's metaphorical field of inquiry and authority. Environmental history courses urge us to delve into scientific fields such as biology, ecology, and even physics, and we should do so purposefully and deliberately. Recognizing this affinity between disciplines requires contextualizing the use of science and its history within your course. This in turn can provide an important dialogue among students with very different reasons for taking environmental history. Environmental history courses will attract students who specialize in scientific fields or environmental studies, and it behooves us to make sure that we consider not just how science informs history but also how history informs science. After a whirlwind tour of Peru, this chapter considers these issues.

As an illustration of the potential of teaching in the field and outside the traditional classroom, let me take you through one example of how a sustained, combined field course might feel. For three consecutive years I taught a month-long course in Peru on the history of nature conservation in conjunction with a course on tropical biodiversity taught by an ecologist, Miles Silman. These history and biology courses were separate on paper and in their formal assignments, but in practice they intertwined. Each day was different depending on where we were and where we were headed. We traveled by plane, bus, boat, and even horse, and our lodging ranged from hotels and hostels to huts and tents. We might go birding at the crack of dawn and then discuss a primary document over breakfast. After morning hikes or botanizing, we could visit a pre-Columbian archaeological site or a market. Meals were prime time for discussions, sometimes over candlelight, and occasionally we watched historical films huddled around a computer screen. Most evenings we discussed literature: first a scientific journal article, usually a study conducted where we were staying, and then a history or anthropology article. The subject matter intersected through the topic of conservation.[1]

With a dozen students we sprinted through Peru's spectacular environments. Our field ranged from the Atacama Desert, the driest place on earth, where it rains less than two millimeters each year (roughly the same amount you sneeze), to the Amazon rain forest, one of the wettest places on earth, where moisture circulates ceaselessly. As much as these natural landscapes revealed biological processes, they also exposed the interface between nature and culture. On the Pacific littoral students learned to identify shore birds and observed the crumbling infrastructure from the late nineteenth-century guano boom, when bird excrement formed Peru's top revenue export. We discussed articles describing how policies shifted from conserving the valuable birds that produced guano to protecting the fisheries that can now be turned into fishmeal protein.[2]

From the coast we went up and over the high Andes, observing mountains terraced into tapestries from centuries of grueling labor. The stark beauty of the landscape brimmed with evidence of complex human decisions, from the exotic eucalyptus wood piled along streets for sale as heating and cooking fuel to the native *oca* tubers laid out to freeze-dry in the frigid high-altitude air. We ascended to the Inka heartland of Cusco, where the tremendous stone works of Inka masons were overlain with intricate Spanish colonial churches. Central Qorikancha remains the most spectacular; the holy Sun Temple had been grafted into a Dominican monastery in the sixteenth century, but a 1950 earthquake crumbled the colonial edges and exposed the dark and ancient glory of a curved Inka wall. Much of what we observed had a clear and complicated resonance within both human and natural systems.

Next we dropped steeply onto a treacherous and breathtaking road through the cloud forest into the Amazon Basin. Here we identified the rain forest products that shape the modern world despite their distant origins. Coca fields stretched out, quietly exposing their storied use in domestic and foreign ... uh ... let's say recreation. Rubber trees stoically bore the cruel legacies of slavery associated with the latex trade. And we go on, through mahogany, oil, gold, and cacao, to examine the waves of extraction that draw upon tropical commodities. Each product inhabits a fixed place in the forest and also on Wall Street. Tangled human stories expose the ways in which societies pluck these products out of their biological context. Rain forest history stretches far beyond its immediate natural context, but in the field that context stands out in a way it wouldn't within the bounds of four walls.

The core of the course was ten days spent at Cocha Cashu Biological Station, in the heart of Manu National Park. Once we made it there, travel stopped, and students learned how research stations work and why they exist. They walked the hundred-kilometer-long trail system observing the forest and read and debated forms of conservation policy. Students designed their own scientific research experiments and executed them: taking censuses of caimans in the lake, estimating the rate at which spiders weave webs across trails, observing primates' behavior. Many began to outline their history paper, due three weeks after we returned home. After a whirlwind of travel, this long stay at the station allowed students to get into a rhythm and observe and understand their surroundings more acutely.

Field courses require a plan and, often, an exhausting pace. A field course requires building creative assignments into a dynamic classroom over a sustained period of time, all the while remaining flexible. Thick course binders worked as our guide and itinerary. The binders included primary texts from the Inka chronicler Guaman Poma and the Peruvian political philosopher José Mariátegui, interspersed with the latest scientific articles. Students carried the binder and a few books, making computers (and the often fickle and hard to acquire electricity needed to charge them) unnecessary. We asked them to read Shawn Miller's *An Environmental History of Latin America* and John Kricher's *Neotropical Companion* before the trip. Each brought the field guide *Birds of Peru* and a good set of binoculars. At the outset they were given three intertwined questions to consider as the basis of their final paper in the history course: How have Latin American peoples understood the natural world, and what meanings have they given to its conservation? What are the ways people in Latin America have made decisions about the earth's biota, and what have been the results for social and economic development? How and why have different plants, animals, or ecological systems stimulated different methods of conservation? Multiple times a day answers, and more questions, emerged. As the course progressed, I worked individually with students to refine the questions to their specific areas of interest for each student.

We matched readings to the places they described. Students identified orchids on the road to Machu Picchu, where we discussed the lawsuit between Yale University and Peru's government over artifacts removed from the site, asking, Just who owns this patrimony? We drank coca tea to ease our high-altitude headaches while we read Bolivian president Evo Morales's editorial "Let Me Chew My Coca," which asks why the alkaloids in coffee are globally acceptable while those in coca are not. As we canoed down the Rio Madre de Dios we read Aldo Leopold's lamentation for this same river, one he had only ever seen on a map, and debated his hope that no road would ever sacrifice its wildness. On day 3 of the boat trip, since there is still no road to reach the inner park, students gain a sense of the enormity of the Amazon and what wildness means in different natural and cultural contexts. Such dialogues captured the connective learning that occurs in the field.

Untethering students from computers contributed to honing their skills of observation. To deepen this I required them to keep journals. These were places to record reactions, meditative thoughts, species lists, and more. I offered prompts for their journals, giving students something to write about tied to the objectives and readings of that day. For instance, after we walked Cusco's central plaza and read Helaine Silverman's analysis "Touring Ancient Times," I asked them to write about how the past is visibly persistent in the present. Before screening the 1974 Brazilian film *Iracema*, a "fictional documentary" about Amazonian development and cultural change from the perspective of a young woman coming of age, I prompted students to write about the different metaphors that explain human relationships to nature. I tried not to overstructure the journals, emphasizing instead that the journals were their own primary documents. In this way the journals became places to record personal memories — of what they felt when we spotted a jaguar strolling along the river bank — or inventories of where, when, and how they identified birds and plants. Some drew landscapes, others affixed souvenirs, but nearly all appreciated the built-in reflection that journal writing entailed. One year I had students pull three of their journal entries and enter them into a course blog upon arrival back home so that we could juxtapose their different versions of the same events. Journals recorded individual observations, but the course structure also lent itself to collective observation, especially as we learned to identify flora and fauna and landscape features. Spotting animals in a dense canopy and describing to others where they sat developed observational and conversational skills. Many of the best spotters were poor describers; practice and teamwork became necessary. Honing these skills, relevant to both biological and historical knowledge production, helps students to develop habits steeped in experiences.

In addition to the sophisticated set of binoculars, the binder full of readings, and the personal journal, students were required to bring a keen openness toward the ways knowledge is produced. Biology students learned a lot about the promise and problems of field research, about the societies and cultures of the places we visited, and about the kinds of contextual and perspectival questions historians ask. History students watched and participated in the process of how science is produced and refined. This comparative exercise was transformational for me, and for many students. It is one thing to critique the colonial attitude of early modern explorers who came to the rain forest naming and claiming all the living things in sight, or to lament the corporate motives of Chevron's geologists.[3] It is quite another to walk through a tropical forest in awe and try to make sense of what you see. We cannot downplay the role of science in imperialism or economic motives for knowledge accumulation, but neither can we dismiss the motive of attempting to understand how the many species in a tropical system fit together for the sake of knowledge itself. This is a crucial place where science helps complete the training of environmental history students by offering a promising seed to match our critical hatchet.

Team teaching makes fieldwork soar. Perhaps the most enriching and serendipitous part of combining these classes was what the professors each learned from and contributed to the other's course. The biology professor asked probative questions in our discussions of commodities, and I attempted, alongside the students, to observe the differences between *Gynerium* and *Heliconia* clusters so that I could see the nonrandom patterns of succession on the river's edge. In this way students and I came to understand what happens in this tropical nature after a disturbance by learning to observe and identify its individual facets. This type of learning — seeking a dialogue with the land itself beyond the library — is crucial for environmental history students and teachers who seek to identify and understand human and nonhuman forces of change. Fieldwork cannot replace the deep reading, persistent searching, and juxtaposition of perspectives historians draw upon to understand human and environmental change, but time spent in the field, with nature in its rawer forms, and in conversation with scientists adds immeasurably to the toolkit on which historians draw. Certainly, many fields of history and other academic disciplines can and do benefit from interdisciplinary and study-abroad courses. My point is not to dispute this but to champion the type of purposeful and deliberate exploration of the field (nature) and other fields (especially scientific ones) that is not nearly common enough in environmental history classrooms.

There are lots of risks and barriers involved with a field course, let alone an international one. High costs, persistent dangers, worried parents, inevitable delays — each one alone could be a reason not to go. The content hours are intense and the planning tasks endless. My best advice is to contract out the travel logistics to local professionals, if at all possible, and gather a good team to deal with the inevitable illnesses, lost passports, and annoying detours. This was easy for me because the ecologist I taught with had been working at the field station for twenty years. He knew who could solve difficult logistical issues and what planning was necessary; I merely appended my course to his itinerary. Starting from scratch would have been much more difficult. But I am certain that the curricular and life lessons far outweigh these burdens. Each time, and for all involved, the course was exhilarating and exhausting on a whole new level.

What if you can't take students to the most far-flung, wildest places on the planet? Nature can be up the road; it is not necessarily half a planet away. One way to consider how to get into the field is to think about your campus as the field. The campus of Boise State University is an urban campus by any definition, but it also sits alongside the Boise River, and just across this river is Zoo Boise. This means that one hundred feet from the History Department students can stand on a bridge over a living (but dammed and channeled) river and see two giraffes in the flesh (and in captivity). Both of these opportunities are easy field trips for environmental history courses.[4] For example, I have been planning a course titled "The Anthropocene: Our Human Age," taught with a geographer, where we might lead students on a silent, ten-minute walk along the river, instructing them to record everything they see and then write up a short reflection. Students then could exchange their reflections, make a master list of what was observed, and classify the list into rough and superficial categories of nature and culture. Are the giraffes natural? Is the river? One could repeat the assignment in the penultimate week of class, but rather than attempt to categorize their list, one might ask students to consider what disciplines are connected to each observation. The idea would be to consider forms of expertise we've built upon all semester and to see what changes from the start of the semester to the end.

Does your university sit adjacent to a city park, or is it surrounded by public lands? Walk that park as a lesson in observation where students record what they see. Take a guided tour of a water treatment plant, visit a botanical garden, or ask the biology department to allow the class access to their avian or invertebrate collection. As more courses go online (or even partially online), the challenge of getting students out of their homes let alone into the field becomes more formidable. In an online class on political history, which was structured around issues of public policy, I made one of the assignments for students to visit one of the public lands sanctuaries around Tucson. Tucson is bookended by two districts of a national park (Saguaro National Park), one of the only cities in the United States of which this is true. Additionally there are state parks, Bureau of Land Management parcels, and millions of acres of national forest land within a thirty-minute drive of the University of Arizona. Asking students to take time from their studies to go be in that public land and think about the history behind the decision to designate the land as "public" is worth a bit of time away from technology and more formal study. For this particular assignment students were actually thankful for the excuse to have to leave their computers behind and immerse themselves in places where some of the most important policy debates confronting the U.S. are occurring.

We have given several ideas for how to go into the field, but in addition to that meaningful and powerful pedagogical choice, environmental history courses would also do well to bring the field into the classroom. Make space for science in your history course. We've been repeatedly asked if environmental historians assign scientific articles as referential knowledge or as texts for critique. We do both. Science provides information, but good historians need to understand how scientists arrived at that information and be able to critique the process. Part of the complexity of assigning scientific studies in a history class is that many scientific articles are written in the opaque language of their discipline or utilize methods that students are not trained to understand. Yet this could also be said about many historical articles. As with most good teaching, the trick is finding readable and debatable content in order to accomplish the skills you have in mind. Exposure to, but never unthinking acceptance of, scientific ideas is a basic goal of our environmental history courses. But we can do more.

One of our consistent learning objectives is for students to take expertise in various forms and apply it to their own questions. A careful consideration of scientific questions, methods, and processes allows us to work toward this goal. We might ask, How do primatologists determine what monkeys eat? How do botanists collect and count species? How do chemists trace persistence? In other words, how do other disciplines *know* things? And to understand the how, environmental historians must learn to read science—nature writing, natural history, as well as articles in journals such as *Science* and *Nature*. Students learn to read science by, well, reading it. This is a crucial part of what environmental historians do; we become literate in a scientific field that informs our chosen topic so that we can learn from it and critique it. Ecology, ornithology, chemistry, hydrology, astronomy, forestry, and botany come immediately to mind, but there are many others.

This can be done in all sorts of ways, but it might begin with familiarity with a given discipline and its publications. For a graduate course I teach called Science, Technology, and the Environment, I aim to have students learn how to synthesize the ways human-caused changes to the planet have been complex, contested, and yet understandable. I have them profile award-winning articles from various scientific journals in a reading-in-the-round session, where students read one article carefully and report on it to the class. Then I have each student select a different influential journal (I provide a list but do allow some flexibility), and I ask them to characterize the contents of that journal over the past thirty years: What has been the most common issue under study? Where is the geographical bias (both in terms of authors' locations and study sites) of the journal? Who has published the most articles? Whose voices appear to be missing? This mirrors a more standard historiographic survey of a topic, where we might expect students to classify schools of thought and directions of inquiry, only its base is written by scientists and it requires students to read a lot of articles (or abstracts) and to at least gain familiarity with the larger structure of those journals. Both help students to become familiar with scientific practitioners as historical actors.

One practical result of having students actually or metaphorically go into the fields of science is that they begin to see how scientific research is conducted. This understanding provides a crucial counterweight to the multifaceted deconstruction of scientific authority. Some students in the humanities come into our classes eager to point out the flaws and the fallacies associated with scientific modes of thought—theories change, data can be manipulated, different genders and cultures ask different questions, and the list goes on. If these critiques emerge, then we've done well!

But it is also our responsibility to convey to them the complexity of formulating questions that science *can* answer and the importance of these kinds of questions whose answers contribute mightily to our collective understandings of the world. One role for environmental historians is to strike a balance between accepting the knowledge the scientific method creates and acknowledging the limits of the process as bounded by society.

One way to do this is to consider the lives of individual scientists. Rachel Carson is a beautiful example that combines all sorts of social context — she's a woman, she did not have a PhD, she died of breast cancer — with contested scientific authority. When Carson dared to ask the crucial question "What has already silenced the voices of spring in countless towns in America?," most of her challengers were other scientists, especially men who worked for chemical industries.[5] While Carson's ecological view posited that humans were a part of the natural world, powerful experts who controlled research science labs and technology argued that they could keep humans separate from nature and, by extension, the effects of pesticides. Political cartoons from the era crystallize these divisions by portraying Carson as a witch or alternatively as a gas-mask-wearing, fly-swatter-wielding Amazon woman taking on the chemical industry.[6] Carson was none of these, of course, but she was a trained biologist who asked a critical question of a public eager to listen.

It is not only our students who might absorb some of these lessons. While humanists commonly acknowledge today's current crisis in the humanities, supposedly evidenced by dropping enrollments and declining funding, we rarely acknowledge shifts and changes that have occurred in the STEM disciplines that also reverberate in our halls. That is, scientists face much greater political scrutiny, from the Left and the Right, on their research and especially their findings.[7] GMO skeptics, climate change deniers, antivaccination crusaders, and others highlight the routine nature with which ordinary citizens call into question the process of producing scientific knowledge and the conclusions scientists reach. Carson and others can help us to draw historical lessons about the right to question scientific authority and also reserve respect for the rigor of scientific practice.

The other side of this (supposed) crisis in the humanities is, of course, that students should also take away a sense that no science is neutral, no science is ahistorical. Scientifically minded students are often the first to lapse into environmentally deterministic explanations for past events. Take climate, as we did in chapter 3. From a purely meteorological perspective, climatic events, especially droughts, might be understood as tragic but natural. To correct this misconception, discussions of climate refugees or famine victims need to demonstrate the ways regimes of power have been complicit in starvation, displacement, and suffering. This is a case in which scientific perspectives must be broadened to include attention to politics and economics. A text that suggests how to avoid this trap is Mike Davis's complex, polarizing, but teachable *Late Victorian Holocausts: El Niño Famines and the Making of the Third World*.[8] Davis combines three forces — climate, world economy, and new imperialism — into a theory about how the modern world was born. He argues that the global inequality that came to be identified with the Third World is a product of the ways these forces combined in a grinding and hastening pattern in the late nineteenth century. He argues that millions of people died in the process of being forcibly incorporated into financial circuits, conditions of production, and terms of trade that confiscated local autonomy and weakened their ability to respond to crises in areas around the world, including India, Brazil, and China. Davis is not a climate scientist, and one might complicate his narrative by locating and introducing more recent understandings of El Niño. Or one could add newspaper articles from the era, as they make up his main sources, to provide more flavor of how people at the time interpreted the crises. However you choose to complement the story, what matters is that students, especially science majors, emerge with an understanding that rather than a scapegoat, climatic change should be viewed as a catalyst that amplifies already complex human relations.

Environmental history cultivates an enormous capacity to see beyond a desire for one true narrative. But what does one do with a stream of stories? The challenge is to cultivate techniques that help make sense of the multiplicity of views and embed them in the appropriate context. We can go to that context (the field); we can read about that context (science); and we can combine both with the practice of history. These experiences foster informed individuals and creative leaders poised to find better ways to steward our earth in the future and contribute to a healthier and more equitable world. If you can, take your students into the field or encourage them to go there on their own. The results are life-changing.

Chapter Six

The Land

SENSE OF PLACE, RECOGNITION OF SPIRIT

TAKING STUDENTS into the field can teach them about an important topic in many environmental history courses: sense of place. Once students have experience traveling to a new place and really thinking about it, the sense of place in environmental history might be easier for them to grasp. If field-tripping is not in the cards for your course or your students, fear not! With the advent of digital technology, including Google Maps and Google Earth, students have a variety of ways to know what is out there. But it is important to note that *there* is not the same *there* as it was in 1995, when the *Economist* declared the death of distance.[1] That journal may have been overstating things, but certainly *there* is very differently understood in the twenty-first century than it was even a generation ago, and it is important to be aware that our students' senses of place and even of history have been radically altered by the advent of communication technology.

Before we can discuss how to teach students about sense of place and recognition of spirit, we must consider the demographic sector sitting in our classrooms and their relationship to place and space via digital technology. Generally college and high school students range from fifteen to twenty-nine years of age. Through the twentieth century, faculty in the United States could anticipate the majority of these students coming from rural backgrounds or at least from families who were at most one or two generations removed from agricultural livelihoods. Today 80 percent of people in the United States and 54 percent of people worldwide live in an urban area.[2] This urbanity shifts the way humans understand the nonhuman world. Rivers flow underground. Ski slopes exist indoors in the middle of a metropolitan desert city. Food grows imperceptibly and appears magically on shelves in stores. Even the vagaries of the weather can be avoided by going inside to escape wind, heat, cold, and precipitation without having to do much labor at all (such as building a fire or patching a roof).

Additionally 90 percent of all those in our students' age demographic in the United States own a smartphone and are using at least one social networking site.[3] Sites like Instagram and Snapchat allow students to connect visually with people all over the world. In many ways our students go on virtual field trips daily, and this ability to virtually travel through others' experience is changing the way they see the world. Their imaginations are developing through digital technology (albeit often in a painfully superficial and filtered way), and thus their senses of place are dependent, in many ways, on what they see through their screens. Jane McGonigal, author of *Reality Is Broken*, provides evidence that "there are more than ½ billion people worldwide playing computer and videogames at least an hour per day. The younger you are the more likely you are to be a gamer. The average young person racks up 10,000 hours of gaming by the age of twenty-one, that is, twenty-four hours less than they spend in a classroom for all of middle and high school if they have perfect attendance."[4] These games often present alternative realities where one can raise a cow (FarmVille), take over civilizations cooperatively with friends (or at least collaborators) around the world or even in outer space (Artemis, Borderlands), or just spend hours lining up pieces of candy (Candy Crush). No matter the content of the games or the networks, our students' senses of place and their relationship to distance, geography, and people are radically altered by these digital and urban realities.

How do you teach a generation for whom distance really might be dead or for whom the wild is something they've never actually experienced? How can we explain to a group of students whose understanding of place is both vast and limited that places have had specific meanings? With students whose lives are increasingly encased in handheld electronic devices that allow friends and families to *always* be *here*, how do we teach about *there*? These questions might make the teaching of historical senses of place and the importance of the spirit of geography to past peoples seem rather formidable, but perhaps it is precisely because of our students' practice in imaginatively traveling, whether through status updates or gaming, that this aspect of environmental history is one of the easier ones to teach. In this chapter we offer ideas of both methodology and content for incorporating senses of place into environmental history units and courses.

The first task in helping students understand the importance of place is to understand what *you* mean by sense of place.[5] The academic definitions of this vary. By *sense of place* we mean the attachment that stems from living in a particular place. We also mean the idea one has about a location far away that one has a sense about but with which one has no real experience. The geographer Yi-Fu Tuan defines sense of place in his masterpiece *Topophilia* as the affective bond between people and place.

Blending these definitions might be the best way to give students the most holistic picture of the importance of geography and place in environmental history. For example, in the 1950s the U.S. government began atmospheric testing of nuclear weapons at the Nevada Test Site. Officials chose the area for its desolation and distance from population centers.[6] While it is true that the region was sparsely populated, it *was* populated. Having students grapple with the fact that bureaucrats in Washington had a radically different sense of that place than the American Indians who called the region home or even the Mormon ranchers who lived a short distance downwind from the testing sites offers a historical example of both Tuan's definition of topophilia as being in love with one's own place, and the more pedestrian, but still important, definition of sense of place as an understanding (or misunderstanding) of somewhere far away.

Bringing the theory to some sort of grounding in the present is essential because it gives students a model for seeing how theories might be applied in practice. I like a jazzy, quick read or even a YouTube video for this. Perhaps no one is better at this in U.S. history than Jennifer Price when she writes about Los Angeles. In "Thirteen Ways of Seeing Nature in Los Angeles," Price takes a literary trip through LA that makes the reader struggle with the variety of places LA contains. She begins the piece with two quotes that serve to bookend her later discussion of her own sense of LA as both paradise and anguish. Steve Martin, she shows us, describes LA as "this other Eden, demi-paradise, this precious stone set in the silver sea, this earth, this realm, this Los Angeles." By contrast, Mike Davis suggests that "the entire world seems to be rooting for Los Angeles to slide into the Pacific or be swallowed by the San Andreas Fault."[7] This article can help students begin to understand the constructed and varied nature of senses of place in a highly accessible and quick reading. In addition there are two compelling (albeit somewhat sleepy) TED Talks that can get students thinking about senses of place in the here and now.[8] Asking students to write their observations about these sources or having a comparative discussion if you've asked small groups to read different chapters in Price's piece or watch different videos can help the material come to life in the classroom. Then you can hone in on the class's operational definition of sense of place for the unit or lesson.

Once you have defined sense of place with your students, the next step is to make the ideas historically tangible. Because of electronic media, our students have decidedly different senses of place than the generation before them, for whom physical location could not be as easily transcended. Our students also may not feel any particular attachment to their locale, and they may have more acutely developed (although not necessarily more accurate) senses of place about the faraway than any generation before them. For these reasons it is important to encourage them to become aware that the biases and preconceptions they bring to a study of sense of place are not so different from those that historical actors brought. One way to do this is to have students read a primary source that is propagandistic and as such is rich in descriptive detail about a particular place and contains the author's affective attachment to (or detachment from) that place. I have used excerpts from the British explorer Robert Beverley's 1705 treatise describing colonial Virginia and William Bradford's description of the "hideous and desolate" wilderness of New England to get at this idea of bias and purpose. Beverley verily bursts with enthusiasm over massacred American Indians and the "Edenic" landscape of Virginia (no mention of malaria or dysentery, of course). Bradford displays an intense fear of the forests and the native nature of colonial Plymouth. We analyze the purpose of these documents (one is to promote Virginia to would-be settlers, and the other is to promote the omniscience of the Puritan God), but in the end it becomes clear that the way the authors sell the place and the potential treatment of the environment is largely based on their sense of the locale and their purposeful relationship to it.

Along similar lines I have had students read mid-nineteenth-century diaries of Oregon Trail emigrants to compare their feelings of the homes they left with the spaces through which they traveled and the environment of the Oregon territory in which they ultimately settled. Here students find the travelers bringing their expectations of the pastoral settings from the Midwest to the arid land of the intermountain West. Many of these travelers insisted on "making the desert bloom" because of their sense that godly spaces must be filled with growing things as well as their affective longing for home. Here a gendered analysis can be particularly poignant, as women's gardens contributed mightily to making the eastern settlers feel at home in the wilderness.

For a course with a longer chronology or a global scope, there are few genres more revealing of sense of place than travel writing. These are a classic source for teaching multicultural encounters among people, but many traditional texts also contain more about place and environment than is typically acknowledged. Adding a few questions about place deepens the observations that Marco Polo made of landscape features and animals during his encounters in Asia. Employing the biography and travel descriptions of Zheng He, the Chinese mariner who commanded expeditionary voyages for the early Ming dynasty to Southeast Asia and even the horn of Africa, students might consider the vast range of places he visited.[9] One of the most transparent encounters comes in early European descriptions of the Americas. I assign sections of Gaspar de Carvajal's account of an Amazonian expedition as the Spanish attempted to navigate and understand the Amazon and Orinoco river basins.[10] Carvajal's text can be opaque, but it formed the basis for a 1972 Werner Herzog film, *Aguirre, Wrath of God*. The first fifteen minutes of the film depict a group of conquistadores descending a steep Andean mountain into the Amazonian lowlands. The Spaniards — priests, soldiers, and mercenaries — and dozens of coerced highland Indians attempt to carry two women in covered chairs down the mountain and through the jungle. The lush, wet, and unforgiving forest stalls their horses and rusts their armor. In vivid color we can see the divide between Spanish objectives and their growing but still quite naive sense of this new place.

Whenever I teach about movement into new spaces, I try to have students read sources from those who were already there. In the example of colonialism of the Americas, it is important to have students read sources from indigenous people (for example, Sitting Bull), whose sense of place was radically different from the settlers'. These sources are difficult to find and very few have been digitized. Most of the sources we find in anthologies relate to the military and biological warfare that the resident peoples experienced during colonization. While these sources are certainly an important part of the historical record, they do not lend themselves well to a discussion of place. It is worth the search, though.

Even finding Anglo sources that articulate sense of place takes some doing. An excellent example of this is the diary of the Nebraska traveler Gilbert Cole.[11] He paints in vivid detail the awful experience of traveling along the Humboldt River in Nevada. It grabs the imagination of the students and helps them realize that even profound dislike for a place shapes how individuals interact with its geography and people. This deep dive into thinking about how hatred informs policy and practice can then be applied in a world history course to think about colonialism or even rescue work. How might negative depictions from colonizers inform Western approaches to regions like East Africa if the environment is depicted as desolate, impoverished, and dangerous? From here discussions of power can unfold as sense of place drives a purpose that is often reactionary, exclusionary, and violent.

Take the idea of wilderness in nineteenth-century America. As Anglo, elite advocates came to embrace the idea that "in wildness is the preservation of the world," spaces that once symbolized danger became idyllic, exceptional, and in need of saving.[12] Here a foray into art history is useful for students; the images of Hudson River School artists such as Albert Bierstandt, Thomas Moran, and the photographer William Henry Jackson allow an opportunity for students to learn to read images as primary sources that can provide profound insight not just into how landscapes and nature existed but also how they were perceived by the chroniclers and the public. A case study of the efforts to preserve Yosemite and Yellowstone helps students understand that identities (national and personal) form in relationship to the nonhuman environment. Additionally these stories, especially if paired with a secondary source like William Cronon's "The Trouble with Wilderness" or an excerpt from Mark David Spence's *Dispossessing the Wilderness*, demonstrate for students that conservation can be as much about politics and power relationships as it is about saving species and ecosystems. Indeed, as those early nineteenth-century Anglo activists sensed the need to preserve landscapes, their nationalist and narrow visions excluded American Indians, who viewed the same spaces not as natural retreats from an overly modernizing world (somewhere to visit) but as home (somewhere to stay). These two senses of place came into profound conflict, which persists to this day.[13]

Once we have investigated numerous examples of what sense of place looks like in historical sources and have settled on a definition or two, I ask students to write their own diary entry about their sense of place. They can write about *any* place; it does not have to be the outdoors. You would not believe how many write about their bedroom. If we get almost no entries that could be considered "environmental" in the more traditional sense of the word, I have them collaborate on an entry about the riverbed that runs through Tucson. The best way to do this is to use Google Docs or some similar software application (see chapter 10 for more ideas). The Rillito River, like almost all rivers in southern Arizona, no longer flows on the surface except during high runoff or after hard rains. The students' entries usually involve descriptors like *barren*, *dusty*, and *inhospitable*. Their dislike of the riverbed is eerily similar to Cole's entries. We then have a discussion about the emotions that a place like that elicits in students, who often posit that it is hard to love or care about a place from which one feels alienated. Perhaps, I suggest, that's why people do not seem overly interested in restoring the river.

By this point students are starting to understand how important perceptions about place can be in motivating people's actions toward that place. But teaching about *historical* senses of place can still be tricky unless you capture their imagination. That is why, after we have spent a couple of class periods setting the scene on our study of sense of place, I like to continue our historical discussions with a larger story. For example, to begin a unit on the geography and environment of the U.S. West I have students examine excerpts from John Wesley Powell's diaries from his 1869 trip down the Colorado River.[14] Powell traveled down one of the most remote rivers in the continental United States and was one of the first (if not *the* first) Anglo-Americans to experience the Grand Canyon. As the one-armed Powell floated in wooden boats in the tumultuous Colorado River, the Ute tribes were beginning negotiations with the U.S. government. These negotiations continued for many years; some would say they continue now. But in 1869 both the Ute Indians and Major Powell were interested in and dependent on the same territory and the same land, although they understood these places very differently. The Ute's cosmology held that earth was the center of all and that each animal had gifted the tribe knowledge and life. Powell brought with him the vision and ideology of an Anglo-European scientist whose culture held that no one had adequately explored the Grand Canyon or the mighty Colorado River, nor brought it under human control. Powell had keen interest in the arid region he was intent on documenting, but he had almost no understanding of the people who had lived there for centuries.

As he gathered information on the flora, the fauna, and the geology of the region, his sense of the place and affection for the unique region became intertwined with his sense of wonder at the native people's historical successes in living in and adapting to the arid place. Through his journey, Powell learned to have a deeper understanding and appreciation of both the nonhuman environment and the humans who lived there. This story allows the classroom teacher to have students practice all kinds of academic skills, from map reading to primary source use (Powell's journal entries are excellent) and ethnography, all in pursuit of the empathetic reasoning that leads to the conclusion that different places have deep meanings for different people, that human beings and the environment are created in relationship to each other, and that all geography is imbued with cultural significance of one kind or another.

As is probably obvious by now, teaching sense of place is essentially teaching intellectual history, or the history of ideas. Topophilia is, at its core, an intellectual concept. In the United States major currents of ecological intellectual thought have included the vast variety of cosmologies of hundreds of American Indian groups; the African-infused sense of place of Africans and African Americans in the slave South and beyond; the Spanish, Hispano/a, and Latino/a layers of topographic claims to Aztlán as well as their migratory experiences; the rural sensibilities of Anglo farmers and ranchers (which differ according to region); as well as the ideas of such elite Euro-American thinkers as Emerson, Thoreau, Muir, and later twentieth-century environmentalists, to name a few.

Because intellectual history is difficult for many students, stepping into the intellectual aspects of environmental history is intimidating, gratifying, and essential. For many students, your exploration of the history of ideas about people's senses of place will be their first exposure to this area of the profession. Settling on the most accessible examples of sense of place, in whatever region you are studying, is best. Perhaps you want to juxtapose native understandings of the tropics with the understandings of colonizers in nineteenth-century Asia. Maybe you want to have students explore the debates around the reconceptualization of the commons in eighteenth-century Europe.[15] No matter which area or time you are studying, it is important to focus on an issue or topic for which a few accessible readings can be put into conversation with one another. The building of the Hetch Hetchy dam in Yosemite National Park and similar controversies offer tidy microcosms with which to see fluctuating intellectual currents of thought about nature's proper role in human cultures and humans' changing ideas about the highest and best use of natural resources. In the case of the Hetch Hetchy controversy in the early twentieth century, the activist John Muir was the preservationist bent on protecting the wilderness for aesthetic and spiritual purposes. His writing alludes to transcendentalist ideas of the valley as a cathedral (a trope that appears over and over in American intellectual environmental history). Mayor James D. Phelan of San Francisco is the quintessential conservationist in the vein of a Teddy Roosevelt who argues that the conserving of resources for future use (such as water in a reservoir) should be Americans' focus versus protecting resources from any use at all. The female activists on the East Coast sided more with Muir in their conceptualization of the Yosemite region as a vast outlet for weary, overly industrialized souls—a respite necessary for soothing the irritating world of industrializing America.[16] When I couch intellectualism as a means for argumentation, I find students are willing to struggle a bit more with it. Thus the selection of sources is important in allowing students the best kinesthetic experience of engaging in a role-play so that they actually have to think and argue as the historical actor they choose to be. Anytime I assign a debate I ask for submission of a formal essay in advance, which outlines students' main ideas and plans for argumentation and rebuttal. This helps ensure they walk into the debate prepared. And I *always* make sure there is some reward for winning the debate to inspire the competitive spirit. Infusing the seemingly dry and complex content of intellectual history with role-playing can whet the appetite of even the most intellectually timid students.

By grounding the learning of intellectual conceptualizations of place over time in controversy, we can also build a nice foundation for moving into a unit on current environmental politics and social justice movements. These are, of course, profoundly informed by worldviews and senses of place, and as teachers of history it is our obligation to give students the skills to make sense of these struggles for power and justice. Historical thinking asks students to take into account multiple perspectives, seek and analyze varied sources, pay attention to context and culture, weigh the evidence, and create an original and sophisticated conclusion about the story that all of this information tells. When done well, instruction about sense of place and the importance of culture and time on those senses of place will teach students these skills. To then ask them to do research on a current debate can be a very effective way to encourage the application of their newly honed historical thinking skills to current public policy dilemmas.

Environmental history's attention to sense of place has historically been applied to *nature* as traditionally defined. Conservation, preservation, the change of natural places over time, and the changing relationships of people to the nonhuman world and how they conceived of those changes are the usual stuff of this aspect of environmental history. Even sense of place histories of environmental justice tend to focus on land and resources. But environmental history can also be incorporated into studies of urban spaces and historic preservation. If you teach about the rise of tenements in the Gilded Age United States or the slums of mid-twentieth-century India, incorporating a discussion of the perceptions of those spaces by the immigrants who made them home, and the middle-class reformers who condemned them, can be fruitful avenues for understanding urban landscapes as places worthy of environmental study.

Historic preservation is rarely considered an appropriate topic for environmental history, but in many instances that preservation is nothing *but* a sense of a particular place. Battlefield monuments and memorialization are particularly poignant examples. For instance, in *A Misplaced Massacre*, Ari Kelman ably shows that memory of the geographic location of the Sand Creek Massacre was skewed over time as the land where the massacre occurred was not adequately commemorated at the time. When the National Park Service finally decided to create a National Historic Park for the massacre, the Arapaho and Cheyenne descendants claimed oral history knowledge of the precise location of the massacre, which the Park

Service quickly dismissed as inaccurate. Here we can see not only a diversity of opinion on the meaning of the event in question (Was this event a brilliant military victory or a genocidal massacre?) but also a disagreement on the legitimacy of sources and an inconsistent memory of the massacre's exact location. As Kelman explains, "Federal officials dismissed Native perspectives on the geography and cartography of a tribal tragedy" as they went about creating the site.[17] Here we see contested meanings over place and the memory of a war-torn environment. Memory of what happened in a place often drives the sense people have of that place. The windswept plains, covered thickly in grama grasses and lonely shrubs where Sand Creek is located, meant something different the morning after the massacre to both the native people whose lives had been shattered and to the scattering of white settlers whom the U.S. Army was ostensibly protecting. Thinking about how that landscape's meaning shifted in that one violent moment and how it changed over time as the memories and the grass grew over the site can subtly shift our understanding of environmental history itself and can make it more inclusive of events that are more often covered in traditional courses.

One can incorporate environmental history into other types of violent shifts by investigating the effects of violence or war on landscapes and people's understandings of them. For example, the decision of the Japanese in Hiroshima to preserve the Genbaku Dome (which was left standing after the U.S. military bombed the city at the end of World War II) in the midst of a peace park can be used to help students understand one culture's use of symbols from the natural world to signal hope for peace and healing. The area now known as Peace Memorial Park was an urban district called Nakajima during the Edo era (1603–1868). It remained a thriving commercial center where goods coming up the rivers on boats were unloaded and sold. In the Meiji era (1868–1912) it was the political, administrative, and commercial heart of Hiroshima, an urban space that represented the economic and political vibrancy of the city. At the time of the atomic bombing, about 6,500 people lived in the neighborhoods surrounding the Nakajima district. In the five years after the bombing, government officials, artists, and residents worked together to remake the area into a memorial dedicated to peace.[18] The decision to make the once commercial center into a pastoral park offers an opportunity for students to think about the significance of war and nature and what catastrophic violence does not just to life on earth but to humans' understanding of their purpose and place on earth. The event and monument also revived traditional understandings of connectedness between the natural world and the nation-state in rebuilding. The Hiroshima Peace Memorial Park can be nicely paired with the September 11 Memorial at Ground Zero in New York City. In this lesson I ask students to research and read oral histories recalling the violence experienced in both places and write essays that compare the ways in which the architects of both memorials utilize elements of the natural world to remake the spaces and transform them from war zones to captivatingly beautiful sites honoring the victims and their descendants. For students researching Ground Zero that might mean discussing the importance of water or of the survivor tree, while those researching the Hiroshima memorial might emphasize and analyze the role of cranes in symbolizing hope. Through such comparisons students can understand how specific moments in time can dramatically shift the meaning of a space and transform the sense people have about the place and the role nature plays in memory, culture, and healing.[19]

For millennia agricultural labor is one of the most intimate ways in which human societies have understood place. Comparing agrarian iconography or pastoral art among places and times can help students see both continuity and change over time in human relationships with the land. Liana Vardi's excellent chapter on how artists' interpretations of peasants' work at the harvest changed significantly in early modern Europe is one secondary source I have used to think about the ways perceptions about manual labor shifted.[20] She argues that from the sixteenth to the late seventeenth century, depictions of peasant labor during the harvest changed from a focus on the work as backbreaking to leisurely and bucolic scenes. Students enjoy pondering the historical context that may have led to a shift in how harvest labor was experienced by the peasants. In particular the production of a sharper and lighter scythe in the Ottoman Empire may account for work becoming easier and its depiction as such in high art. This is similar to and can be engagingly compared with the increasingly positive depictions of forests in European culture by the mid-1800s (perhaps explained by the increasing scarcity of woodlands because of the overharvesting of lumber) or the arrival of and infatuation with agricultural technology in mid-nineteenth-century American art (especially McCormick's reaper and John Deere's steel plow). While agricultural art and iconography may not represent popular understandings of place, they can provide a compelling glimpse into the ways in which nature and a culture's emotional attachment with certain landscapes depend on humans' physical experiences.[21]

Our students gaze upon a vast landscape of varying places through the screens of their computers, tablets, and phones. They get lost in make-believe places where they experience a reality they cannot live. This positions them to be able to imagine places far away and in the distant past, but they need to be guided in that imagining. Lessons on senses of place give that imagination accurate historical underpinnings. In teaching students to think about their own place and in helping them recognize that places can have radically different meanings that shift over time as a result of significant events, we can emphasize empathetic reasoning while we reinforce the important concept that the environment is not an easily and consistently understood entity. What constitutes an environment shifts meaning in different cultural and temporal contexts, and those meanings have very real implications for cultural legitimacy, political decision making, and distributions of power.

―― *Chapter Seven* ――

The Power

ENERGY AND WATER REGIMES

I FIRST HEARD OF Auditor from my brother when I was in Montana doing research for my dissertation. Legend had it that the shaggy dog with canine dreadlocks lived in the famous Berkeley Pit mine of Butte, Montana, eking out an existence in a severely polluted place where life seemed next to impossible. Workers on the night shift put out food and water for the dog and built him a shanty doghouse.[1] He shunned human contact, leading miners to respect his toughness and solitude. They named him Auditor because he routinely showed up when least expected.[2]

I went to Butte to try to see Auditor. I didn't see him on that first visit. I did, however, see the Berkeley Pit for the first time (and I would see Auditor on many visits after that). There, on the hill above the quaint mining town, sat the foreboding lake of toxic water born of intense copper mining operations over the long twentieth century. The water is noxious enough to dissolve metal and lethal enough to kill unsuspecting birds that stop over, as proven dramatically when large populations of migrating snow geese succumbed to the pit in 1995 and again in late 2016.[3] The water-filled pit looks deceptively peaceful, in a moonscape without a blade of grass, tree, or shrub. At the time of my visit in 2002, residents of the town were watching the water level in the pit rise from runoff and lived in fear that it would soon overflow and bring a river of contamination into the town.

The Berkeley Pit is a particularly intriguing example of how water and energy are deeply connected in the environmental history of the American West and the world. In designing an environmental history syllabus or unit, one could focus just on water or just on energy, but linking the two offers instructors and students alike an opportunity to see beyond boundaries as these two megatopics connect in important ways with other environmental history subjects. Food, climate change, and environmental justice, to name a few, are inextricably linked with water and energy. Much like an ecosystem, the study of discrete subjects in environmental history often blends into other topics and even other disciplines (as we discussed in chapter 5). By taking on water and energy simultaneously and unveiling their deep influences on one another, students can begin the complex process of grasping the power of connectivity in the past and in the present.

Let's begin with energy. As humans in a transnational capitalist economy participating in consumptive practices, we and our students are using energy in amounts unprecedented in human history. The food that we asked students to intellectually engage with in the first few days of an environmental history course (see chapter 1) is, in its essence, energy. When our students turn on their electronic devices to travel virtually to new places and environs, they are using energy. The use and harvesting of the sun's power for electricity requires energy. Mining fossil fuels for power requires energy. The flora and fauna in wilderness require energy. Energy is part of every endeavor and pursuit, even politics. As we listen to debates about the "end of oil," about drilling in the Arctic, about subsidizing renewable or clean energy, the headlines are peppered with one of the most urgent environmental policy issues of our day.

Another issue that has emerged as urgent for human survival in this fragile era is water. Water and energy are ecologically linked in important ways. The sun provides the raw energy necessary for plants to photosynthesize, but the process would not happen without water. Plants are 90 percent water, human beings 60 percent, and the earth's surface is 71 percent water. Water is as much a requirement for life as is energy. Both of these resources demand endless debates over the world's future, and they have compelling historical narratives that are relevant in any conversation that involves finding solutions to the impending shortages of both resources. These narratives are too often left out of traditional history courses. But whether you are designing a stand-alone environmental history course or taking the hatchet to one of your other courses, these two topics deserve inclusion.

As if these reasons weren't enough, there is one more reason to consider using energy and water as the spine of your environmental history syllabus or as a major topic of study in your world, regional, or U.S. history courses. That reason is simply that water and energy enable teachers to center the nonhuman environment and, if not decenter human beings totally, at least place them in a context that demands acknowledgment of their dependence on the earth's natural resources. By now, we hope, it is clear that environmental history, at its core, is the study of changing relationships between people and nonhuman environments over time. But a lot of what we have discussed so far has *people* at the center. Our chapter on the hatchet asks us to consider and critique how humans have changed on different timelines. As chapter 6 shows, historical understandings of senses of place reveal how different people have conceived of the nonhuman world over time. Food is certainly about how humans' decisions and choices affect nature near and far. And when we unmilk the llama we are still focusing on what humans didn't do.

What's missing in a lot of these discussions (and is often missing in my own classroom, much to my dismay) is the functioning story of the nonhuman world itself. Julie Cruikshank asks the provocative question "Do glaciers listen?" in her analysis of oral tradition and scientific knowledge in the Yukon and Alaska.[4] But it is admittedly very difficult to teach from the perspective of a glacier or a tree. Still there is a way to center nature in your course design. It takes enormous discipline and forethought. Historians are not inherently predisposed to decenter humans. Indeed, if we do, we fear it might lead to an overly simplistic conclusion that the environment determines the course of human history, something with which most historians are uncomfortable. Considering nature at the center also forces us to admit our lack of expertise. We suddenly must know and be able to explain at least a bit of chemistry, hydrology, and geology in addition to history. But if we are to get our students to truly empathize with the nonhuman, putting the environment at the center of the story, at least part of the time, is worth doing when we design our courses and lessons. Water and energy are ubiquitous and broad enough to take center stage as we try to decenter humans and recenter the environment.

Let's begin by centering water. I choose to begin the course or unit by asking my students to do research on a river of their choice. I give them a list with several options, and I allow them to choose one that is not on the list with which they may have a particular connection. When I am teaching environmental history, the U.S. survey, or a U.S. West course, I put the usual suspects on the list: the Colorado River, the Hudson, the Mississippi, the Rio Grande, and so on. (I exclude the Columbia; you will see why toward the end of the chapter.) But I also throw in a few extras, such as the Chicago and even the Cuyahoga River. This is a fairly rigorous assignment: I ask students to research the river's geography, history, and current economic importance. I require them to put that information into the historical context of the place(s) through which the river flows. I give them temporal parameters based on how I have structured the chronology of the class, which varies with each course. The writing assignment is "Think Like the River," for which they must write an autobiography of the river's life.[5] I tell the students to write with "readability" in mind and offer them prompts to consider which parts of the river's life were the most interesting, controversial, tragic, or triumphant. We then host a book club, where each student reads another student's work from the perspective of a nonhuman member of that river's ecosystem. In this rendition of role-playing, students imagine what nature's agency might look like. This lesson helps them to find empathy with the rivers they study, and it's a great way to get a sweeping overview of the health and history of

America's rivers. Obviously the lesson could work beautifully in a world history class as well; the Nile, Congo, Orinoco, Amazon, Danube, Rhône, and Yangtze offer wonderful possibilities.

The Colorado River can serve as a specific example of a riveting story emerging from the complex details. A student will discover that the river begins its life high in the mountains of Wyoming and Colorado from the runoff of snow in some of the most beautiful mountain high country in the world. It was born as a result of massive mountain building events (the Laramide Orogeny) and tectonic uplift (of the Colorado Plateau) and knew its current life by about 5 million years ago. It has been fed by generous and stingy tributaries alike, and, in its early life its primary labor was canyon cutting and watering high country forests, semiarid deserts, and ultimately the Pacific Ocean. By at least one thousand years ago it contributed to the irrigation of human crops, and by the eighteenth and nineteenth centuries the river supported permanent human settlements and transportation. But perhaps the twentieth century is the most formative for this relatively young river. Students will discover that, increasingly, humans put higher demands on the river that affected which fish swam its waters and which animals and plants had access to it. Indeed the Colorado River Compact of 1922, in which humans divvied up the river's contents among six very different states and two nations, and the damming of Glen Canyon in the 1960s might be two of the river's more challenging moments. In the twenty-first century the river is powering coal plants and being diverted across the Sonoran Desert to a faraway place named Tucson, where it refreshes humans, waters golf courses, and even recharges an aquifer. It is responsible for nourishing a large metropolis that it has never seen (Los Angeles) and gives of itself to support millions of acres of agriculture and provides tens of millions of people with potable water. This river might very well be exhausted in the students' rendering of it. Or it might be heroic and strong. Whatever parts of the story the students choose to include and whatever interpretations they decide to offer, others in the class will learn the vast complexity of rivers and, by extension, an introduction to water history. By completing this assignment, students will, we hope, realize that thinking like a river is useful for attempting to understand the environmental history of that precious and increasingly unavailable resource.

From there you can go in many directions with your content and instructional focus. To recenter human effects on water availability, I ask students to consider the fact that water does not exist solely in rivers. It lives in laws, in our imaginations, and in very real distribution structures. Using a specific law to put a different perspective on water (a commodity as much as an ecological agent) is an effective instructional choice. I find the U.S. West's doctrine of prior appropriation—better known as "first in time, first in right"—to be particularly compelling for opening up debate and helping students begin to understand the reality of scarcity and shortage and the legal ownership of this essential resource. Complex legal topics are opaque when presented in lectures and can be inaccessible if presented only in readings. I find that tangible and concrete kinesthetic demonstrations are effective in helping students to see the law and thus to understand it. When discussing prior appropriation, for example, I bring in a big cooler of water, an empty cooler, and a pitcher of water. I give each student in the demonstration cups on which I've drawn a line and written a date (for example, April 24, 1871). When classes are small, all students can participate, but in a larger lecture setting you can single out seven or eight students to take part in the demonstration. I set the water cooler on a desk and put the empty cooler just underneath. I then have students fill their cups to the line. Students who have earlier dates get their fill; students with much later dates get less. When the cooler is full of water, everyone gets the amount they are allotted, but then we do the exercise again, this time with the cooler about half full. It works out that those downriver or who have junior allotments (later dates on their cups) do not get their full allotment. When I simulate rain by pouring water from the pitcher into the cooler, some folks who didn't have water get a little. We then evaluate the problems with the system and discuss the ramifications of drought or overuse by people with earlier rights.

Even if your focus is not on U.S. water rights law, you can still utilize a simulation similar to this one to encourage your students to think about the conflicts and compromises surrounding this shared resource.

Useful for a global approach is Sara Pritchard's notion that the Rhône River's channelization and industrialization represented a "confluence" of ecological and technological systems.[6] Perhaps you can focus in on Saudi Arabia or other desert nation-states and compare or contrast the ways they have approached water distribution historically. Authors such as Donald Worster can help prod your students to deeper analysis no matter the geographic focus of your study. Especially helpful is Worster's notion of dams and other water-control mechanisms in arid places as tools of empire. His thesis is not dissimilar to Karl Wittfogel's famous "hydraulic hypothesis"; I have paired excerpts of both in a debate setting in order to compare the creation of centralized, bureaucratic, technocratic, and authoritarian governments in different water geographies (China, Saudi Arabia, Germany, and the western United States, for example).[7] The essence of the debate is to decide whether or not we can reject or accept Wittfogel's thesis. This lesson might work particularly well in a comparative politics course or an introduction to world history course.

One of the great characteristics of environmental history is its capacity to connect various approaches to history. Water is a perfect conduit for this learning objective. Water allows us to bring the history of labor, politics, race, gender, and technology to bear on a single place or moment in time. Take, for example, the construction of dams in the United States. After the passing of the 1902 Reclamation Act, the United States embarked on half a century of remarkable dam construction. The dams ostensibly contained water behind them and conserved it for future use while also generating hydroelectric power as, theoretically, a clean and renewable source of energy. The building of specific dams, such as the Hoover Dam, is replete with fascinating stories about river ecology, industrial labor, technological engineering, special interest group politics, and masculinity and the related twentieth-century mentality of dominance over nature. In many global examples of dam building, issues of inequality come to the forefront. In postindependence India, dam building became an essential part of the country's plans for development.[8] Construction of the dams along the Narmada River in western India, however, led to political tumult as peasants waged protests and launched lawsuits. Again environmental history allows us to ask interdisciplinary and vitally relevant questions. In the case of dams, we learn a variety of answers to the question of how governments have balanced the competing needs of different constituencies. And we can then ask how they should do this moving forward with ecosystems and biodiversity in mind. In this way dams can highlight the rise of environmentalism if one focuses on the recent decisions to breach some dams. The Elwha Dam in Washington state, whose destruction can be viewed on YouTube, is a fascinating case. In all of these examples the unyielding concrete structure of a dam brings the topics of water and energy together in compelling ways.

Rivers provide only one compelling conduit that can guide your course, and it is worth pointing out the obvious: that water topics extend far beyond rivers. Ice, floods, hurricanes, oceans, and countless other geographical features and phenomena include water. Irrigation, drinking water, recreation, and other uses also come to mind, as does the appearance of water in literature, song, and even cinema. Because water is essential for all life on earth, it has a deep history and a relevant present that promotes engagement, analysis, and debate. All of this can lead your students into meaningful projects around local water problems and solutions. Asking students to gather information about the local situation and using a variety of problem-solving assignments can serve as a perfect summative assessment about water's history and current reality. In a capstone cross-disciplinary project that focused on water, I asked students to work in collaborative groups to create a variety of solutions to our arid city's impending water shortage. If you have students in your classes from all over the United States and the world, they can either work on a similar project individually or gather in groups of like interests. The point is simply that water and energy both allow us, as history educators, to seize the opportunity to have our students *apply* their historical knowledge and thinking to a contemporary issue that requires them to engage in creative ways with real problems.

As students take on the history of water in your courses, you can weave the topic of energy into the lessons. For example, not only does it take energy to clean and distribute water in the modern world (especially in arid places), but water is itself one of the earliest forms of energy utilized by human beings. The other compelling justification for pairing these two current and controversial topics is time. If your chronology is such that the bulk of your course is devoted to modern or contemporary time, these topics may characterize the age (especially after you have hatcheted more traditional timelines).

The nineteenth and twentieth centuries, in particular, have been dubbed the Energy Centuries, and the post–World War II era witnessed what the historians J. R. McNeill and Peter Engelke deem the "great acceleration."[9] Pivotal changes in energy regimes unfolded across the globe, and in those two centuries energy and water became ever more inextricably linked. If we zero in on the most important raw elements of energy and ask our students to bear in mind the elements' relationships to water, the inseparability becomes obvious when they read, write, and research those relationships. There are excellent sources on the energy and water connection, but getting just the right collection of readings does take some cutting and pasting or copying and scanning.

I privilege the histories of the fossil fuels coal and oil (carbon), but I also offer lessons on alternative sources of energy such as uranium as my elements of choice for the case studies for energy in a U.S. survey or an introductory U.S. West course (the students ultimately broaden their knowledge of different energy sources, particularly wind and solar, during the end of the course or unit project). I usually have students report their research in a shared document so that we can gain a quick (albeit superficial) introduction to that material and move toward the intersection of human uses of the element.

If you have decided to focus the entire course on water and energy, you can create significant units of study for multiple sources of energy. If not, you may zero in on the one you think the students will find the most relevant. I sometimes let the energy source most often in the headlines dictate what we study. For example, when clean coal was a significant issue in the 2012 presidential election, we spent quite a bit more time on coal than on other energy sources so we could arrive at a rigorous understanding of the historical underpinnings of coal energy. Students likely use electricity every day that is largely produced by coal; once they know that and discover that tens of thousands of gallons of water are required to produce one megawatt of electricity in conventional coal plants (ones that use once-through cooling), the relationship of water to clean coal becomes very obvious.[10] There are also case studies of the ways in which coal and water become more closely linked in the twentieth century, when coal comes to be used to move water across vast, dry distances as in the Central Arizona Project or to power desalination plants in California and Israel.[11] The key is simply to choose the narrative (I prefer thematic over chronological in this case) and be sure to emphasize the natural processes and resources involved in such coupling.

When pressed to make a choice, though, the thematic narrative I choose is oil. It is full of political intrigue, presents interesting opportunities to engage in cultural history, and is consistently in the headlines and in our lives, which allows students to own the content. The other beautiful part about using oil history as a fundamental component of my syllabus is that it can help with that hatchet part of the environmental history course design process. Energy history, through the eyes of the energy and not just humans, makes the traditional narratives students hear about certain people and periods look very different. The story of J. D. Rockefeller is particularly gripping and is a perfect example of a narrative that shifts profoundly when focused on oil and not on his wealth. I usually show a segment of Daniel Yergin's documentary *The Prize* because it brilliantly depicts Rockefeller's innovative understanding of the nature of oil and its usefulness while also highlighting his utter disregard for the ecological ramifications of its use.[12] Rockefeller emerges from this sort of study as a rather ordinary product of a particular moment in America's environmental history when utilitarian use of the environment overrode most of the concerns for human health and the well-being of the earth. His vast economic empire begins to look rather tenuous from an ecosystemic rather than an economic perspective.

America's (and the world's) cultural love affair with the automobile also changes when examined through the lens of the energy required to manufacture and propel it. Thus when car culture is paired with energy history, the Model T becomes a polluter and energy hoarder and not just the machine that remade gender, race, and geography.[13] Stories from the headlines, difficult political choices made daily in institutions of government, and examples of environmental activism form compelling parts of this narrative. As Keystone XL and the Dakota Access Pipeline and the catastrophic BP oil spill have become matters of public awareness and debate at various moments in the past decade, the long history of oil pipelines becomes essential to know. For instance, the story of the Alaska pipeline is a useful historical topic to ground your students in pipeline history, as is the story of Nigeria and the Niger River Delta (see example in chapter 8). Pipeline construction and use have taken dramatic tolls on both the ecosystems and the human communities, so they offer students an opportunity to consider the trade-offs required of the fossil fuel–powered consumerist economy after World War II.

Water is central to most of these topics, especially as they manifest in the present. An immediate visual connection of oil and water comes to mind — think of the Deepwater Horizon drilling platform in the Gulf of Mexico or the *Exxon Valdez* spill in Prince William Sound in 1989.[14] The water to which we refer is marine and can take the class discussion from freshwater drinking sources to the world's largest ecosystem, the oceans. If you have time, here is a wonderful place to insert a unit or lesson on climate change and the effects of greenhouse gases on the polar ice caps, the levels and temperatures of the oceans, and the powerful changes in weather patterns that result from the fossil fuel energy regime. Climate change is nothing if not the intersections of energy and water.[15]

Climate change is so scientifically complex that younger students may not be ready for that discussion. Instead I offer them a hidden water story in the fossil fuel culture in which we are all complicit. The water required to produce just one gallon of upgraded crude oil from tar sands, for example, is around 4:1 (four gallons of freshwater to one gallon of crude). Add another two gallons to take the crude to gasoline.[16] The history of this technology adds more dimensions for discussion. It takes 36,000 gallons of water to manufacture a car, for example. However you approach these topics, students will be engaged because the topics are relevant and current. Having students apply their learning to evaluate the decision to build the rest of the Keystone or Dakota Access pipelines or drill for deep-sea oil asks them to reconsider the received narrative of economic essentialism. (Namely, the idea that we must build and drill in order to propel economic growth.) When looked at in an environmental history course or unit, the interconnectedness of oil and water reveals that these debates are not just about jobs and economics but include and are limited by very real ecological factors that should be considered.

The Atomic West is another rich repository for highlighting the connections between water and energy. Uranium processing and mining requires abundant energy, and the surface flow of rivers in the U.S. West, especially the Columbia and the Colorado, have been particularly important to the growth of atomic America as a global power in the mid-twentieth century. Using primary sources and excerpts from the collection *The Atomic West*, we examine the broad environmental ramifications of that uranium and atomic development.[17] When I teach the survey, I include a fascinating study on the Oak Ridge National Lab in Tennessee. If I focused on the U.S. West, then we turn to readings about the Colorado Plateau, Hanford, and of course Los Alamos in New Mexico. This comparison can be made global with anecdotes, readings, or a lecture from Kate Brown's masterful parallel history of two communities—one in the United States and the other in the Soviet Union—that became havens for individual families working in nuclear settings.[18] Plutonium production, a filthy, hazardous process leading to nuclear weapons, emitted immense loads of radioactivity, leaving hundreds of square miles of uninhabitable territory. To entice workers into jobs in this risky production, U.S. and Soviet leaders both created orderly, aspirational communities of prosperity, places Brown dubs "plutopias." In both places government officials spent lavishly on schools, recreation centers, and consumer-oriented shopping facilities giving the workers and their families access to these amenities they otherwise would not have had and helping them to overlook the inherent risks of their work. Brown explains the common features that reveal what the atomic age meant to the working people building bombs in landscapes transformed by the process.

After a broad investigation into uranium as an element of energy (both destructive and constructive), we return at the end of our class to rivers, where I ask students to consider the probability that the cold war was won thanks to rocks and rivers. This assignment requires students to reconceptualize their original river's contribution to nation building by comparing the extent of industrialization that their river has undergone with the story of the Columbia River. We get at this by reading Richard White's brief but potent book, *Organic Machine*. The idea that by the mid- to late twentieth century rivers had become cogs in an industrial energy system has a mind-opening effect on my students. In short, I ask the students to do independent research and chronicle the industrialization of their original river in much the same way that White does with the Columbia by writing an essay that has sections that emulate White's.[19] I ask them to consider first how the lens of labor changes how we view nature. Second, they consider the river as being put to work. The power of the river is the transition to energy for humans, so the students must also consider the fish or other organisms that inhabit the river. Once their comparative research is done, we spend the remaining class time narrowing in on the story of the Columbia as both water and energy. This study continues to put the environment at the center of the story—as a player in global politics, as a vital resource with multiple users, and as a constantly changing home for flora, fauna, and people.

The binary of nature as existing independently of humanity (or, more commonly, vice versa) can be upset by centering the environment in the stories we ask our students to engage with in environmental history courses or units. Water and the raw elements of energy can be the conduits for the deconstruction of this binary. Human dependence upon natural resources is effectively revealed when we center energy and water.

And so it makes sense to return to Auditor the dog in the Berkeley Pit. Despite the fact that he never let miners touch him or even see much of him, the employees of the mine left Auditor Alpo dog food every day, sustaining their canine mascot for years. Auditor lived on the largesse of a species that was willing to pollute its water sources in order to produce the raw elements of energy required to make the Alpo and become a world political and economic power.[20] In the end the copper, which was once mined from the recesses of the now water-filled pit, sustained both Butte and Auditor. As Auditor lapped freshwater from his dog bowl, he lived in the human-constructed landscape that interconnected energy and water in ways that can never be uncoupled and certainly should never be disconnected in any rendering of their history. Not far from the pit lies the Marie Mine, a closed uranium mine that has been reclaimed by the Bureau of Land Management in order to protect nearby water sources, and in the northeast corner of Montana lies the Bakken Oil field, which holds an estimated 4 billion barrels of oil — all of which is only accessible using water-based hydraulic fracturing. These are significant reminders that the energy landscape in which Auditor lived his life remains vitally and intimately connected with the present and future water regime in the U.S. West. This story is true, in different manifestations, the world over. Auditor died in 2003, after more than seventeen years in the pit; I can't help but wonder if he wasn't at least somewhat aware of the irony and the importance of the place he called home.

PART III

Applications

IT SHOULD BE CLEAR by now that the potential number of topics in environmental history and the connections among them are nearly limitless. If water and energy don't work for you, water and climate might. Or disease and energy. Perhaps agriculture and urbanization? Maybe the field of science is not where you want to align your course, but religion, art, or literature is. In this section we offer three specific and more technical applications for environmental history that belong in every course. We see these as overarching concepts because they are not specific to certain topics (although they can be discrete topics of inquiry) but are fundamental and essential to the functioning of a classroom, whether or not we choose to grapple with them.

Traditional narratives, even of environmental history, very often told stories of a world that was too wealthy and too white to resonate with the lived experiences of most people. Attention to many voices and encounters with the environment can and should expand the reach of environmental history despite the difficulties of excavating these voices. Along different lines, historians might elect to ignore the abundance of new technologies for teaching out of allegiance to past methods, or out of fear, ignorance, or very real time constraints. We aim to provide motivation and examples for why environmental history might convince you to take up Twitter. Assessment is rarely on the top of our priority lists, despite the wishes of administrators. More often it is a requirement rather than a function of our teaching that motivates and inspires. And yet assessment merits consideration not only to complete the design process but to evaluate and reflect on our teaching practices.

In the last three chapters, therefore, we offer suggestions for ways of incorporating the applications of diversity, technology, and assessment into your course design. Each application requires deliberate forethought for effective implementation and sometimes necessitates coming to terms with uncomfortable challenges facing our classrooms but beyond our control.

── *Chapter Eight* ──

The People

ENVIRONMENTAL JUSTICE, SLOW VIOLENCE,
AND PROJECT-BASED LEARNING

IN THE HOT, humid summer nights of 1978, Robert Burns and his two sons drove along rural roads in thirteen North Carolina counties in a liquid tanker truck with an open bottom valve. Spilling out below, and running into the soil along the road, was a liquid contaminated with polychlorinated biphenyls (PCBs) removed from the Ward Transformer Company in Raleigh. The company's executive, Robert Ward, had concocted the illegal spill plan in part to avoid the escalating cost of disposal.[1] As a result of this poisoning the state had to remediate the 240 miles of contaminated roadside soil. To do so the state devised a plan for a landfill in Warren County, a rural area in the northeastern region with a majority of low-income, African American residents. A small farmer facing bankruptcy sold his property to the state for the landfill site.

But the citizens of Warren County opposed the selection of their home for the hazardous waste disposal. They argued that the disposal threatened their groundwater and would stigmatize the community and harm the local economy. After they sued the state and lost, construction of the landfill began in 1982. So the protesters changed their strategy and argued that their community had been chosen specifically to take advantage of disempowered poor people and people of color. Civil rights activists embraced an environmental perspective while environmentalists expanded their resistance to include concern for the racist ramifications of hazardous waste siting. Unrelenting protests and the arrest of nearly five hundred people failed to stop the landfill. But a larger issue had been broached: Warren County's uprising marked the birth of the environmental justice movement.

This chapter aims to provide two applications for environmental justice in your classroom. First, we discuss the academic and theoretical implications of the concept of environmental justice as well as its historical origins. Using examples from the United States, Nigeria, and Ecuador, we consider how you might apply such concepts in a course with historical material. Second, we consider project-based learning as a way to empower students to investigate environmental justice as a historical topic. Combining these strategies, we hope, provides a glimpse of the many opportunities for taking up inequality and power as core components of environmental history.

Before going much further, we want to explain the context of environmental justice, as it may be a new topic for some. Beginning in the mid-1950s in the second (some would say third) wave of civil rights movements in the United States, marginalized and misrepresented groups came together to demand justice for the indignities and inequities their people had suffered for centuries. Consciousness-raising among women of all colors, the lesbian and gay communities, communities of color, and the poor manifested in very real and tangible political gains. But the environmental movement tended to be mired in elite, white demands for wilderness and wildlife preservation. In the late 1960s and into the 1970s environmentalism took a populist turn as clean air, clean water, and safe disposal of hazardous wastes became the causes of the day. Still the idea that the poor and people of color suffered environmental poisoning and pollution far more than elite, white communities would take some time to gain legitimacy in the U.S. cultural and political landscape. Thanks in part to the experiences of Warren County residents and others, a broader movement emerged that challenged American environmentalists to move toward the difficult recognition that harmful environmental practices were often most acutely felt by communities that had been historically exploited because of race and poverty. The movement advocating for this recognition named its position *environmental justice*.

Pairing environmental issues with concerns about inequalities among people can provide the perfect opportunity to introduce the concept of intersectionality by emphasizing race, gender, class, and environment within the context of power struggles that have involved all of those categories of analysis. The framework of environmental justice history provides a platform for inherently more inclusive histories and a way of situating the environment alongside social, cultural, and political histories. Studying the environment together with and integrated into other kinds of history helps to showcase the civic potential of our classrooms. One example, such as the landfill siting in North Carolina or oil extraction in the tropics, can provide an array of opportunities for research, analysis, critical thinking, real-world application, and creative problem solving. And because of the linkages inherent in environmental justice history, it offers opportunities to go comparative and global with your content. In any comparative attempt, one must be careful not to overgeneralize and lose sight of the specificity that makes each case unique. But the desire to be accurate should not scare us away from attempting comparisons. Importantly, comparing environmental justice case studies from around the world should help increase your students' ability to empathize with people from different backgrounds and different circumstances, an important objective for all history education, in our opinion. Asking your students to then transfer their historical learning onto a real-world problem or project will increase the impact of this important approach to environmental history instruction and offer students opportunities to practice the skills that are necessary to approach problems of global environmental injustice.

For newcomers or global specialists, *environmental justice* may seem an odd term. You might be thinking, Why haven't environmental issues routinely included issues of justice? The particular emphasis on justice as a framework for redressing environmental issues is a characteristic of U.S. approaches to inequality guided by pragmatic concerns to correct wrongs, often through legal or governmental channels. In other world regions, environmental movements were not necessarily divorced from social issues, so other political frameworks help explain citizens' concerns. Joan Martínez-Alier has named this the "environmentalism of the poor," and Ramachandra Guha's "third world critique" of environmentalism points to the social consequences of integrating ecological concerns with livelihood and work.[2] Vandana Shiva has long pointed out the intersectionality of biodiversity, indigenous rights, and women's rights. Some researchers have termed the emancipatory potential of political activity focused on the environment and natural resources "liberation ecologies."[3] Scholars from others fields, such as Noel Sturgeon, are often doing some of the most engaging work in complicating the "politics of the natural."[4] In Latin American historiography environmental histories often begin with social rather than legal, political, or cultural questions.[5]

While each of these frameworks might help a global class reach a consensus about environmental burdens, I find Rob Nixon's concept of "slow violence" the most powerful. Nixon has suggested we take account of the pace and brutality of environmental burdens placed on the poor by calling them "slow violence." Although it is a rather self-explanatory phrase, Nixon specifies that he means the sort of attritional violence from delayed destruction that occurs gradually and is typically not viewed as violence.[6] Rather than immediate, explosive, and spectacular events, many of the most destructive environmental calamities play out over a range of temporal scales that render them invisible. For the mostly poor and geographically marginalized people who experience nuclear tests, chemical spills, and industrial poisonings, slow violence creates an emergency of global proportions yet one happening at a glacial pace so that it rarely earns notice. For students, slow violence can be a way to consider deep questions about justice itself and develop empathy for comparative experiences.

So how do you teach this? The seeping detritus of oil drilling near the Equator can be combined in a comparative study that allows students to grapple with slow violence.[7] I've had success pairing two parallel stories about oil extraction's lingering effects in twentieth-century Nigeria and Ecuador. In both places international oil companies began drilling mid-century with little regard for the toxic effects of the process. Indigenous peoples and minority communities bore the brunt of poisoned lands, and brave individuals spoke out about the effects. Both crises came to public awareness in the 1990s but were the product of decades of oil history. For the Nigerian case I primarily assign readings from the prison diary of Ken Saro-Wiwa, an Ogoni activist who began fighting against the Royal Dutch Shell Oil Company in Nigeria and who was later hanged for his activism. For Ecuador we view the documentary *Crude*, about the lawyer Pablo Fajardo and the Ecuadorian lawsuit against Chevron-Texaco requesting it to clean up after oil drilling in the Amazon.[8] A U.S. court levied an $18 billion judgment against Chevron-Texaco in 2011. While not entirely parallel, both cases have a seemingly straightforward narrative of corporate greed and exploitation with native heroes. Students might find these aspects familiar (different geographies, similar struggles, latent injustice), but we are headed toward a deeper conversation about slow violence and what remediation might look like.

First let me give a bit more context from a lecture that begins this unit. The first oil tanker carrying crude from the Niger Delta departed in 1958; since then $600 billion of oil revenues has similarly sailed away. Oil accounts for more than 90 percent of Nigeria's export revenue, and Shell is the largest foreign stakeholder, with 47 percent of the Nigerian oil industry. But financial gain and exports are one small part of what this resource extraction did to the land and the people who live on it. As the profits from oil were funneled into Shell, the Niger Delta homeland of Ogoni people (a micro-minority of about fifty thousand people within a Nigerian population of 140 million) became so polluted as to be nearly uninhabitable. Putrefying waters were made unfit for drinking and fishing, croplands were scarred by oil spills, and air was fouled by natural gas flaring.[9] The ghastly practice of flaring is itself a case of environmental injustice: it involves igniting the natural gas resulting from petroleum production rather than containing it. This activity has shortened the life expectancy of delta peoples, bequeathed a blazing false sun that burns constantly, and released millions of tons of methane and carbon dioxide into the atmosphere. As long as wells were pumping, the gas was burning, at least in the Niger Delta. Nearly 76 percent of the natural gas in Nigeria was flared, compared to only 4 percent in Great Britain and 0.5 percent in the United States. Shell's classist and "racial double standard" was supported by a brutal Nigerian regime that responded swiftly and violently to Ogoni protests against the company by killing at least two thousand people in 1993.[10] The international response was tepid at best.

After establishing this setting, we consider the life of Saro-Wiwa. As an Ogoni writer and activist, he merits our focus for several reasons, foremost because he left an accessible personal record that students can excavate.[11] His story is filled with tragedy. He led a nonviolent movement against Shell and was an outspoken critic of the Nigerian government, which, he argued, failed to enforce environmental regulations in his homeland. In a trial widely regarded as corrupt, Saro-Wiwa and eight other leaders of the movement were found guilty of murdering four Ogoni chiefs within the same movement during a schism over strategy. Dubbed the Ogoni Nine, they were hanged by Nigerian military personnel. Several legal cases were later filed against Shell in Nigeria and in the United States (because the 1978 Alien Tort Statutes gives non-U.S. citizens the right to file suit for torture or extrajudicial killings). Saro-Wiwa's son brought a case that was settled out of court in 2009 with Shell denying liability but agreeing to a settlement of $15.5 million for victims' families.

As a sprawling, indirect, and compelling missive, Saro-Wiwa's diary is hardly a straightforward text, and I rarely have the space in a class to assign the whole thing (about two hundred pages). Add to this the complicating fact that he often quotes at length from his own past speeches and letters, and it becomes a text embedded with just the sort of complexity that merits in-depth discussion. Instead I present students with an abridged version — a single night's reading of about sixty short pages — that we use to understand the processes to which Saro-Wiwa's chronicle bears witness.[12] We begin our discussion by analyzing his tone, style, and voice. What is personal about the account? What is intended for public consumption?

Where do these lines blur? Next we seek out facts that help us understand the Ogoni's situation. These matter not so much for their veracity as for the way Saro-Wiwa employs them as true. We then look at specific parts of the book, the preface plus chapters 4, 6, and 9 that contain narrated conversations, a prison song, lengthy quotes from his previous books, and the Ogoni Bill of Rights and statement of unity. These documents-within-the-document lend themselves to close reading. To tease out this complexity, I write a list on the board of documents that appear in this section of the diary, including his daily routines. I then pair and assign students to identify the messages that emerge from each of these documents. We discuss each in turn and try to understand the kinds of slow violence experienced by Saro-Wiwa and the Ogoni. The paradox of wealth inequality always emerges here, as well as the clear humanity of those inflicted. We conclude the discussion by constructing a timeline that accounts for the years leading up to Saro-Wiwa's imprisonment. This trinity of discussion techniques (individual perspective, layered internal documents, and timeline building) allows us to appreciate the facets of one man's experience and to make sense of the comparative case.

Other mineral-rich equatorial regions have similar stories and heroes.[13] Pablo Fajardo was the lead lawyer in a suit against Chevron Corporation for contaminating Ecuador's tropical Oriente region. First exploited by Texaco (which is now owned by Chevron) in the 1960s, the Lago Agrio oil field produced about $25 billion of oil over the next twenty years. Exploitation left behind open pits, contaminated water, and crude spills, causing chronic health problems. Of Cofán ancestry, Fajardo worked as a kid in Texaco's oil fields and then put himself through law school. He is featured, along with other lawyers, in the 2009 documentary *Crude*. In 1993 thirty thousand Cofán collectively sued Texaco in New York. The oil company repeatedly requested that the trial take place in Ecuador instead, according to the makers of *Crude*, due to a belief that those institutions could be manipulated. The case, and various associated appeals and counterclaims, are further complicated by the changing ownership of the oil field, which was released back to the Ecuadorian government in 1995, allowing Chevron-Texaco to argue that the cleanup is a governmental concern. Celebrities, especially the musician Sting and his wife, Trudy, have publicly supported the Cofán struggle. The film nicely brings these perspectives to bear on the case with striking footage from the polluted lands. Recent newspaper articles and annual reports can be paired with the documentary's story to update and enhance it.[14] Perhaps official documents produced by the oil companies may someday be available as well.

To present these stories I use a shifting mixture of lectures, readings, and films, all traditional techniques. It is useful to assign the diary and film because the stories resonate with each other and the characters are complex. But to have students process and internalize the material I ask them to engage in empathetic imagining. First, I have them complete reverse texts from either men; that is, half the students compose a diary entry as though from Fajardo, and the other half write a courtroom opening statement as though from Saro-Wiwa. This ensures students have models on which to rely, but they must consider different facets of each case. It is a short assignment, two to three pages long, due on a day dedicated to discussing environmentalism and the law. I have several students read their texts aloud. Then we consider the tough questions: Who are the heroes, and who are the villains? Where are the consumers of oil in each story? What does oil exploitation and its consequences say about national sovereignty? How do you compensate people for lost land and culture? What would justice look like? Rarely are students satisfied with these questions, but their answers predict how they will look at environmental harm going forward.

Using the lens of slow violence and the comparisons of Ecuador and Nigeria, Ogoni and Cofán, Saro-Wiwa and Fajardo, I attempt to expand how students conceive of environmentalism on its many scales. Through their writings and their words Saro-Wiwa and Fajardo put a personal face on the environmental struggle. This serves many functions: it humanizes the experience, vocalizes the response, and legitimizes the act of speaking out. But focusing solely on individuals can be counterproductive. In our discussions of individual, collective, corporate, and government responsibilities, I aim to remind students that planetary problems cannot be resolved only by the heroic actions of a few charismatic individuals—

institutional actions have a profound impact on environmental outcomes. It is no accident that lawsuits have become the strategy of choice.

Another way to have students appreciate why environmental justice is significant to understand is to situate it in a discussion about climate change. As we addressed in chapter 3, climate change as a historical phenomenon has enormous potential for classroom instruction. The climate change of recent decades shows us that the poor will be differentially affected by the results. In 2014 the Intergovernmental Panel on Climate Change (IPCC) of the United Nations released its report on the predicted effects of climate change. The authors wrote, "People who are socially, economically, culturally, politically, institutionally or otherwise marginalised are especially vulnerable to climate change."[15] This conclusion is the thesis for any environmental justice unit: that the marginalized are more vulnerable when it comes to environmental dangers.

To get students to understand this injustice, have them brainstorm some of the effects of and solutions for the damage caused by climate change. You can certainly use a specific event (Hurricane Harvey, Irma, or Katrina or drought in Zimbabwe or melting of the Greenland ice shelf) to help make the discussion more meaningful. If you choose a specific event, giving students time to research the event is essential. After they have listed a half dozen outcomes of climate change (think here of rising oceans and disappearing shorelines, increased food costs because of changing weather patterns, higher electricity bills for those living where average temperatures are warming or cooling significantly, catastrophic weather events and the cost of cleanup and rebuilding after those events, etc.), have them brainstorm one consequence for each effect. Realistically not all effects will be negative; certain populations might benefit or at least bear less of the burden. Next have them suggest strategies for mitigating the most severe effects of climate change. Then have them draw a chart that connects the effects with a list of skills and resources required for citizens to access the mitigation strategy. From this you should be able to have students deduce that economically and politically marginalized groups will be hardest hit by the effects of climate change and least likely to be able to access the power networks necessary to capitalize on the strategies of mitigation. This disempowerment has been socially constructed and historically specific; this is why it is so important to teach environmental justice from a historical perspective.[16]

Certainly we instructors can take the more traditional "sage on the stage" instructional approach when we venture into the difficult terrain of environmental justice. We can find four or five of the best examples, lecture on them, maybe even pair them with a few dynamic sources and have a discussion on them, then assess students in a traditional "what did they learn" way. This may be all you have the space to do. But another way to teach environmental justice is to ask students to engage as authentically as possible with the field itself, and thus I am especially intent on making this part of my environmental history courses student-driven.

If there is an area of environmental history that is, at its very core, populist and driven by grassroots mobilization and hard work, it is environmental justice. Maybe that is why I think it is very powerful to have students actually live the process of uncovering injustice and engaging in problem solving to the extent possible in the history classroom. They quickly learn how complex the problems are. They quickly learn how complex the power apparatuses are. They quickly learn to have deep respect for those environmental justice activists who have had any success at all. And hopefully the students learn that it takes a great deal of commitment, knowledge, and grit to ensure the implementation of "urban and rural ecological policies to clean up and rebuild our cities and rural areas in balance with nature, honoring the cultural integrity of all our communities, and [at the same time] provide fair access for all to the full range of resources."[17] Those are the words of the delegates to the First National People of Color Environmental Leadership Summit held in October 1991. With this content area, it is preferable for us to become the guides on the side and allow students to discover the vast complexity of environmental justice through their own research, writing, and engagement. The great diversity of examples of environmental justice allows students the opportunity to practice research, critical thinking, and problem solving through project-based learning.

Project-based learning has its roots in the twentieth-century progressive education movement usually associated with John Dewey. He is famous for saying, "Give the pupils something to do, not something to learn; and if the doing is of such a nature as to demand thinking; learning naturally results."[18] The project is the "doing" part of learning.[19] Most simply, this instructional method allows students to produce tangible products that answer essential questions through research, writing, and critical thinking in a collaborative setting. The best project-based learning is also grounded in real-world settings and asks students to exhibit their work for a public audience. I find constructing projects as problems motivates students.

Project-based learning takes a lot of time and effort in the planning stages, much patience and flexibility in the implementation stages, and ample celebration in the assessment stages. Increasingly school districts, independent schools, and some liberal arts colleges are encouraging teachers to adopt project-based learning as a means for increasing student engagement and emphasizing skill acquisition. Traditional content instruction and assessment are effective and important for some learning objectives, but they are not effective at encouraging student achievement in addressing the complexity of both issues of justice and of environmental change. I find project-based learning to be particularly appropriate for application in the environmental history class because so much of what we study requires deep learning from a variety of disciplines in addition to creative problem solving. Both of those are difficult for an individual teacher to accomplish on her or his own. By engaging students in the process of research, we can require that they reach out to experts in relevant areas to understand a particular environmental justice story, and thus we can cover as much (if not more) content in a more dynamic way. With a topic like environmental justice that has at its core the power differentials of various voices, project-based learning helps to mitigate these discrepancies.

As an example, I have used the Conference Project in a variety of ways in several of my seminars. The basic premise of the project is that the students are to role-play experts who are gathering to shine a light on a set of contemporary issues. I have made some projects very grand and some very humble. In all its permutations, students say they learned more from the project than in any other part of the class. What they produce is also extraordinarily good, and the rigor and depth of learning exhibited in their end-of-project reflection essays are inspiring. I have used this method in my women's history course (as a way to broaden our scope to include global gender inequity), in my post-1945 U.S. politics class (around issues of racism), and in my environmental history course (for environmental justice in particular, but I've also used it for water scarcity).

For maximum clarity and execution, every project has an entry event, an entry document (with an essential question), a performance, and a reflection. The entry event is, ideally, a guest speaker who can visit your class either in person or via Skype to speak about an environmental justice issue in your community or region. In Tucson, for example, that speaker could have expertise in groundwater contamination from the military or air pollution from refining or the inappropriate disposal of mining mill tailings. A video can also work well for an entry event. If you have neither the time nor the resources for either, you can stage the entry event by role-playing one of the key actors. The entry event simply grabs the attention of the students and becomes a key referent.

As far as I am concerned, the key to great project-based learning practices is the entry document, which you should give to students after the entry event. The entry document sets out the project parameters. For the Conference Project, your students will be taking on the roles of expert policymakers for the United Nations. The project is to host a day at the IPCC UN Conference in 2020 (or some future year) where their responsibility is to inform attendees of three (or as many as you want) current environmental justice emergency situations in the world and compare those with similar historical events. You want to be sure there are not too many events because you want the research and discussions to be deep and rigorous. Also you want students to be able to find information on the historical events, and if you require too many events, there is less likelihood of locating adequate research material, especially if you do not teach in a school with a robust research library. If you are teaching U.S. history or another national history and want to avoid the global comparative aspect, you can have students create a policy summit for the environmental agency in the federal government, such as the Environmental Protection Agency.

The essential question for the project can vary, but I generally use the following: What are the most urgent environmental justice issues in the world (or the region or the nation), and what does history have to tell us about how best to proceed in addressing the issues and resolving the injustice? Once you have settled on the essential question(s) that will drive your class inquiry, you can decide whether or not to limit your students' research by giving them a list of acceptable areas, or you can leave it up to the students' discretion. If the project is highly collaborative, setting a parameter of expectations can lead students to where you want them to end up without your having to stipulate each legitimate topic for investigation. And here is where your design of the project comes in. If you want to be sure all continents are represented in the summit, you divide the class into continents. If you want to hit only the developing nation-states of Africa, Asia, and Latin America, then limit the summit to those regions.[20] I am always interested in making sure students understand that it is not just the Southern Hemisphere that deals with these issues now or in the past, so I have students find two contemporary issues of similar topics and have them compare these with a historical occurrence in the United States. Remember: environmental justice can be conceived of encompassing nonhuman nature and its effects on human populations (for instance, water pollution), but it can also be conceived of as including public health, working environments, and industrial health. If you allow students to cast their nets widely, you will have more diversity in the project, but beware that that may make it hard to draw conclusions at the end.

Set deadlines for the summit — both the ultimate deadline and intermittent check-in deadlines. Devote an entire class period for the summit. If you have short classes, use several periods; the discussion will be worth it. The products I ask students to produce have two parts. First, I require students to create websites, which must include a historical synopsis of the topic, a definition of the current problem to be solved, identification of the key actors (including the victims of the injustice) and their points of view or needs, identification of terms required to understand the issue, and an explanation of how and why this is specifically an environmental justice issue. The website must also include a discussion of the strategies that have been used up to this point to solve the problem and an update on where the problem stands now, including links to sources for further reading and contemporary journalistic stories or documentaries.

Second, students are asked to make a presentation to the attendees of the summit. The presentation is structured around the idea that the student is a policy expert who is offering insight into the best means to mitigate the injustice, using examples of successful (or unsuccessful) tactics they found in their historical investigations. This is the part of the project that students will struggle with mightily. Be sure to have individual or group consultations to help them with their problem solving and argumentation. Require student meetings during office hours or during scheduled classes. As we all know, students will try to avoid these meetings, so I build meeting attendance into their grade for the project (you show up, you get the points). Finally, the class is ready for the summit.

To be considered gold-standard project-based learning, the summit should include visitors from outside the class. Invite other professors or grad students. Have the class perform the summit before the whole school or in a public setting. Invite a panel of experts from the community (a particularly powerful choice; you'll be amazed how excited the community members are to help). The point is not how important the outside participants are; just that there is an authentic audience for the students to exhibit their research beyond their own classmates.

All project-based learning should have time for reflection; the best has time for reiteration and revision too, but I often fall short of that. My reflection activity for the Conference Project is to have students choose one of the contemporary examples from their classmates' research on which to write a fairly lengthy essay about how to solve or mitigate the problem, including an interview with their classmate on their opinion or ideas and, if possible, one interview with a real policymaker involved in the issue. For example, one year a student emailed Erin Brockovich, the environmental activist who built a legal case against Pacific Gas and Electric for drinking water contamination in California in the early 1990s, and she responded!

One of the biggest concerns with project-based learning is assessment. Teachers ask, How will I know what my students learned? Project-based learning is the perfect place to combine performance-based skill assessment and content-based assessment. For the difference between the two and an in-depth discussion about assessment in general, please see chapter 10. For now, just know that your objectives for teaching environmental justice will likely have included more concepts than facts. I've described oral skills (the conference), written skills (the website and essay on a classmate's research), and research skills (embedded in the completion of each of these). More specific goals can be devised and communicated with a rubric.

From the polluting of the oceans to the diminishing supply of clean water for the poorest people and to the rising seas and chaotic weather patterns associated with climate change, the twenty-first century promises to require our very best efforts in problem solving. The unevenness and inequality embedded in these problems are revealed through the lenses of environmental justice and slow violence. There are many pitfalls in studying these issues. Race, class, and gender analysis is often a new approach for many students, so spending some time at least introducing those concepts is crucial. The suggestion that the poor should just work harder and move out of the bad environment can serve to demonize the poor in ways that are not only counterproductive to rigorous analysis of structures of economic power but serve to reify the marginalization of the poor. Be ready for this.

In teaching environmental justice through project-based learning, we have the opportunity to offer our students a rigorous experience practicing the skills of research and information gathering, creative and critical thinking, collaborative problem solving, and deep communication. All these skills are required to tackle the most difficult of the environmental injustices in the world. This is a complicated area of study, but the world, and especially those who are stuck in polluted and denigrated environments, requires our students to not only be aware of their plight but have some practice in thinking through solutions.

Chapter Nine

The Tools

USING TECHNOLOGY TO ENHANCE ENVIRONMENTAL HISTORY

THERE IS A great exhibit in the Arizona Science Center in Phoenix that displays a room from 1985. There's a rotary phone, a VCR, a camera, a fax machine, a phone book, a typewriter, an alarm clock, a TV, a calculator, a flashlight, a weather monitoring system, a Rolodex (remember those?), vinyl records, and a radio. The sign under the exhibit captions a photo of a microchip and reads, "Thanks to this tiny chip, everything in this room now fits in your pocket." Many of the teachers and professors in classrooms in the early twenty-first century remember a time when at least part of that room didn't fit in our pockets, but many of our current students (those born after 2000) and all of our future students do not. The year 1985 is also when Donna Haraway published an essay that is now a cult favorite, "The Cyborg Manifesto."[1] In that piece Haraway explored the ways in which human beings were fast becoming cyborgs, a combination of human and machine. The essay was written as a critique of second-wave feminism, but when used in an environmental history course with millennials, the essay leads in new and fruitful directions. Most important, Haraway asks the reader to deconstruct traditional, antagonistic dualisms (such as nature/culture, male/female, machine/human). Haraway argues that historically these dualisms were used as justifications for dominance and oppression. By rethinking these relationships, she argues, everyone and everything can become cyborg, and as a result true liberation (for women, earth, non-human animals, etc.) becomes possible. The logical extension of this is that if humans are not unnatural and nature is not inhuman, then reclaiming both becomes less daunting. When one asks millennial and younger students to engage with that idea, they do so willingly, because they live in a world where the mechanical and the natural are fused to an extraordinary degree. Our students are the digital generation, and they demand and deserve to be taught in ways that match how they learn. To ask this digital generation to both celebrate and critique the development of and dependence on various kinds of technology (from horses to cars to those chips in their pockets) is like watching fish take to water.

But ask teachers to become cyborgian in their instruction methods, and it may be more like watching fish take to land. When we discuss such science fiction concepts as cyborgs, our students cannot just conceptualize this moment in history; they are, in many ways, living it. Our students connect, collaborate, socialize, and think *through* technology. They take photos, create videos, and engage in conversations via texting over sixty times a day on average.[2] They read endless streams and blog posts on Tumblr. On Instagram alone there are 21 billion images uploaded every year, and all of those are just begging to be viewed by our students.[3] They game and binge on Netflix and create their own stories on Snapchat. They imbibe the world through their screens: they learn through technology. And, like it or not, that style of learning must be accommodated if we expect to maximize our teaching effectiveness. This is not to argue that *all* traditional methods of instruction should be thrown out, but it does mean that a new pedagogy for the digital generation can and must include the use of digital media and communication technology. These technologies, when used well, are vehicles that can transport our teaching to a new dimension: one infinitely more effective for and engaging to the digital learners in our midst. In short, we teachers would do well to create a cyborg pedagogy.

Perhaps the best example of the debate around how to teach digital natives involves the question of the lecture. Many of the discussions on pedagogy in a digital age turn on the question of whether or not to lecture. These debates situate the lecture in the noncyborg realm of instruction and tend to argue that lecture is a passive delivery of information from human to human. Even when teachers incorporate technology into lecture, it tends to still be passively used; trying desperately to exert self-control and not sneak a glance at their phones because use of phones in the lecture has been strictly prohibited, students stare at a distant screen displaying traditional text and still images. This sounds familiar to many of us because it is our and our students' daily reality. Many proponents of new digital pedagogies argue that the lecture is (or should be) dead.[4] Others swear that lecture remains the best way to impart essential knowledge. Just as Haraway would articulate a middle way to the dualisms we encounter every day, we believe that lecture can still be an effective and essential way to confer information to students, but there are ways to cyborg our lectures that will be more deeply engaging to the digital generation.

The cyborg lecture is one that asks students to produce during (or immediately after) a lecture rather than just consume the content being given to them. For example, technology can be infused into a lecture to check for understanding. Having students quickly utilize in-class polling applications such as PollEverywhere can give you immediate feedback on the class's collective understanding of a particular part of the lecture, or it can be used to ask students to weigh in (anonymously) on a controversial question or idea. PollEverywhere is not just multiple-choice polling. You can set up polls in advance that allow for open-ended answers. If you have a large number of students in your lecture, you can draw names from a hat and have that small group contribute. You will be amazed how interested their peers are in the enterprise even if they are not directly participating in that moment. Twitter is an application that can be used in a million ways in the cyborg classroom, but one way to utilize it in lecture-based classes is to have students tweet to each other both before and after class. By using a common hashtag for the class (for instance, #areweallcyborgs?), students can tweet questions they have about the reading or questions they still have after class, and you can open up the next class with discussions of those questions. You can have students summarize the lecture in 140 characters or less (this is eye-opening to say the least), or ask students to tweet their favorite information from that day's content. If Twitter feels too public and your school has an online learning management system, use the forum or the discussion tools in the same way. In doing this work you will also be asking students to create a review resource they can use in later course work.

As lecturers we can model critical thinking and use of sources with tablet apps like Adobe Reader and by flipping our classrooms. I have students read and annotate sources in advance of a lecture and share their annotations by email (either with me or with their peers). I then pull up a random selection of annotations that serve as the basis for comparison of different readers' understandings of the same texts. Some instructors are flipping their classrooms by video-recording their lectures, uploading them to a YouTube channel, assigning the viewing of the lecture as homework and then using class time to have students bring in clarifying, critical, and discussion questions based on the lecture. In a flipped classroom, professors and students spend the time together discussing, analyzing, and clarifying content rather than being exposed to it for the first time. Flipping is difficult to do, and many instructors worry that having students watch a lecture and read for homework will overload them, so they prioritize reading (which is easier to do outside the classroom). It should be noted that one does not have to flip the entirety of every lecture in order to flip a classroom. We suggest giving snippets of lectures in video form a few times during a course. Prepare a fifteen-minute section of a lecture and pair it with the primary (or secondary) sources you would like to discuss in class. This also models how to utilize sources in presentations if you hope to have students give their own lectures at some point in the course. If you are new to flipping, just do it once or twice during a course and see how it goes. Try it on! Experiment. The depth to which your students learn that material will tell you whether or not it was effective.

Another fabulous interactive tool for cyborg lectures is the digital sandbox. This is basically an online whiteboard that can be collaboratively edited. (If you use an app such as Twiddla, you can invite your students to the space before that day's class begins.) Uploading an image and analyzing it together or having students take notes as you lecture and then critically assessing the notes are ways to have students contribute to the material you want them to know about while still maintaining the essence of the lecture.

There is one more way to engage students in the lecture: as guest lecturers themselves. Using applications such as EduCreations (for tablets), you can have students create parts of a lecture. For example, if you are teaching about Haraway's contributions to the history of technology, a student can be responsible for teaching Haraway's biography or giving an overview of cyborgs in popular culture over time (Frankenstein's monster comes to mind). They can create a two-minute mini-lecture using EduCreations (or some other collaborative application), or Google slides, VoiceThread, or some other application in your content management system. If you are worried about quality, students can share their mini-lecture with you ahead of time. These approaches do not get rid of the lecture; they utilize the machines in our midst to encourage students to create and produce knowledge and ideas alongside the instructor.

By willingly becoming cyborg instructors, our lectures can become more engaging and interactive, more cultivating of the kinds of skills we want students to hone while they are in our classrooms, and thus more effective overall. Having students create, collaborate, critique, and communicate *during* our lectures will show them the lecture is not a foreign, premodern construction they must endure but an experience in which learning looks like their everyday lives.

The above discussion has, at its core, a very important assumption: that, as teachers, we are not afraid to have communication technology active in our classrooms. In the opinion of many instructors, digital tools are simply distractions that have no place in the classroom, and indeed early adoption of technology for the sake of technology did not always improve learning when it lacked a revolutionary shift in pedagogy. When computer technology first arrived in the classroom, it was usually used to teach the same material *in the same way*. For example, teachers would put lecture materials that had once been on overhead pages into PowerPoint and then use an interactive SmartBoard to link to a website that they used to talk at a largely passive, consuming audience. That was instructional technology for lectures 1.0. If, however, we expect to not only meet our students where they are but also prepare them for where they are going, we must begin to incorporate instructional technology 2.0.

Just as the Web 2.0 has encouraged its users to create and contribute to the information highway rather than just consume static content that is slow to change and relatively unchangeable by the user, so too should our instructional use of technology promote a pedagogy that requires students to design, create, produce, and collaborate as they learn. The best use of technology asks students to communicate their learning to a public (or semipublic) audience. If our assessments are real-world, performance-based, and skill-focused, then our use of technology can and should reflect that bias and further those objectives. Take writing. Formative, problem-based writing assignments can promote learning when students simultaneously evaluate the work (see chapter 10). Ask students to share those assignments with a broader world (via blogs, for example), and suddenly there is more at stake than the individual student's grade. We can even ask students to read each other's essays and make a video representation of the work they can upload to YouTube. Any creative assignment that asks the student author to make his or her writing viewable by someone other than the teacher offers students the opportunity to write while participating in a world of information sharing that is likely familiar to them. Make the assignment collaborative (build in a critique of each student's policy proposals on India's tiger problem, for example), and you begin to make learning social.

The interactive, social nature of human beings (and maybe even cyborgs) seems to be fed every minute of the day with social media applications. Perhaps academia should be the quiet world away from all that noise.

But academia segregates itself at its peril. Instead of fearing or avoiding that world, we instructors of environmental history, at a revolutionary historical moment for both the environment and education, would do well to turn those applications into tools for more effective and engaged learning. Twitter, Facebook, Instagram, collaborative websites and discussion boards, even Google Docs can allow students opportunities to continue the class conversation beyond the classroom walls and long after the time allotted for in-person learning.

Those opportunities that allow our students to process their learning in collaborative ways are the essence of real-world environmental problem solving in the twenty-first century. For example, if your project-based assessment for your water unit is to have students figure out the most effective and efficient way to save the most water in your area, you can require them to use technology in myriad ways. In the first step, ask students to define the problem; research and investigation drives this part of the process. Technology should be used for more than just the Internet as the locus of research. Working collaboratively, students can share sources and research notes using Google Docs. In the next step, designing and brainstorming solutions, students can utilize mind-mapping applications (or they can draw maps of their ideas, take photos of them and upload them to a Google Doc or wikispace for you to see their ongoing work or to elicit feedback and critique from others involved in the project). Asking students to maintain a work blog where they write periodically (weekly seems to be the most effective) about the obstacles, successes, challenges, and opportunities involved in their progress is a way to make collaboration and teamwork public and helps students to be reflective about processes, not just outcomes. In the final phases of the project, technology can be especially essential. Requiring students to use some sort of communication technology in their solution provides them the opportunity to think about the usefulness of various kinds of technology in resource management. For example, in a transdisciplinary project on water conservation called Project: Inquiry, one group of students decided that creating an app for Tucson Water users to access the water quality status of reclaimed water at a variety of residential water quality testing sites could alleviate some of the public's concern about drinking reclaimed water. The students designed the app and presented their idea to officials at Tucson Water (thus completing the last requirement of great project-based learning: public and real-world presentation of student work). Throughout the entire Inquiry project, the students utilized group texts and emails for communication, Prezi and PowerPoint for presentations, Survey Monkey and other survey software for audience assessment, Google Docs for work logs and research notes, video and photo applications, and of course Web 1.0 for research and data analysis.[5] Using technologies in lectures and in projects and assessments lets students participate in the real world, making the intellectual work of the academy relevant in a way that some argue it is ceasing to be.

In short, the software of Web 2.0 and the hardware of smartphones and tablets and computers should inspire us to be cyborgian teachers: educators 2.0, if you will. A good rule to follow is that if your use of technology is allowing only you, the teacher, to use the technology, produce the knowledge, and evaluate the learning, then you likely aren't using technology in a way that is really transforming pedagogy into something that will reach your digital learners. As we suggest in the next chapter, assessments in the twenty-first century would do well to evaluate students' abilities to apply their learning to the production of new knowledge, and technology allows them to do just that. In addition, when so much content is available at a click, learning becomes more about processing and making sense of information than it is about rote exposure to it. As digital immigrants, many of us feel uncomfortable letting go of our control over our students and our classrooms. Technology may represent new frontiers of learning for us. But if we expect our students to understand that learning is lifelong and worth pursuing, we must model that. The incorporation of a cyborg pedagogy in which communication and information technology are essential tools for learning, not simply entertaining distractions, requires us to be willing to learn alongside our students.[6]

Having said all of that, instructional technologies remain simply tools. They cannot replace great teaching; they can only make great teaching greater. The cell phone cannot have conversations with itself; it needs human beings to make it relevant and useful. One of the best intellectual exercises I have ever done with my students is to have them create questions that Google cannot answer. So as we utilize technology to transform our pedagogy and make our teaching and learning of environmental history richer and more dynamic, we should always keep in mind, and remind our students, that a cyborg culture is only as brilliant and ethical and effective as the humans who make it.

Chapter Ten

The Test

ASSESSMENT METHODS, RUBRICS, AND WRITING

LIKE MOST HISTORIANS, we have suspicions about assessment. In her recent article in the *Journal of American History*, Anne Hyde argues that historians "suck" at assessment for a number of reasons, the first of which is that we just don't want to do it.[1] Hyde relates institutional, political, and practical reasons for this discipline-wide inertia, but in the end she concludes that, like it or not, we need to take assessment seriously and get better at it. We agree.

Another reason for our collective skepticism might be the polarizing nature of assessment discussions. There is a train of thought, starting in K–12 education, that what gets tested gets taught and that teaching without testing is ineffective. Many of the best and brightest educators and education policymakers boarded that train in the United States in the mid-1990s and have ridden it through to the recent overhaul of No Child Left Behind. In the past five years, however, the locomotive of high-stakes testing seems to be running out of fuel. Enough critics have demonstrated that not all standards are created equal and not all testing works. Still, the standards-based movement has affected both higher education and the K–12 worlds of education. The buzzword *assessment* and the data imperative are everywhere in our professional circles and are often politicized because there is so much at stake for teachers, students, and society. There is no denying that unanimous agreement may be nearly impossible to achieve on matters of such great importance as what students should know and be able to do, but we believe that one thing we can and should agree on is that assessments, when done well, should promote student learning and growth. When assessments do this, they should be welcome and central components in any course design.

In this chapter we address nontraditional, creative, and authentic assessment rather than focus on testing of either the standardized or organic variety. We offer alternative approaches for both measuring student achievement and advancing learning in environmental history courses. We argue that the best assessments and evaluations do not just check for understanding of some agreed-upon standard of knowledge and skill; they offer opportunities for students to continue learning even as they are assessed. Assessments can be opportunities for students to use real-world skills to apply their historical understanding. The two opportunities we focus on are projects and writing.

Let's start with a little history. In 1956 Benjamin Bloom created a taxonomy of learning that helped to categorize and scaffold the skills that students should be able to use well by the end of their formal education. Educators widely adopted Bloom's taxonomy. You are familiar with it, no doubt. You may even still use that pyramid to help you formulate clear objectives. At the base (and thus the most important) was knowledge, which asked students to recall specific information, especially facts. Next came comprehension, where students were asked to show understanding of that knowledge. Application, for Bloom, meant the "use of abstractions in particular and concrete situations."[2] Educators in K–12 often stopped there, assuming their colleagues in higher education would focus on the final three skills on the pyramid: analysis, synthesis, and evaluation (higher-order thinking skills). Bloom's pyramid reflected a general bias in American educational culture for knowledge acquisition as the primary goal of education. That goal was then assessed as teachers filled the proverbial pail and students passively received these nuggets of knowledge and regurgitated them on command.

In the late twentieth and early twenty-first centuries education theorists began to rethink Bloom's taxonomy. Rather than throw out the approach, though, these theorists simply inverted the pyramid so that higher-order thinking and skills would be emphasized more. Key to the implementation of the categories are the verbs that can be used to ask students to employ the skills: *summarize, categorize,* and *design.* The revised Bloom's taxonomy suggests that remembering information should be the foundation of the pyramid, with the ultimate goal being information's application (using information in a new way or in a new setting), creation ("using information to create or design something new"), analysis (taking information apart, examining it in order to understand it better), and evaluation ("critically examining" the information in order to make judgments about its relative strengths and merit). In between remembering and the top of the pyramid lies "understanding."[3] And it is understanding that most teachers hope students achieve (rather than rote memorization). In the old days many teachers believed only formative tests could prove understanding, but new thinking suggests that many formative tests simply reveal cramming and rote memorization that students forget quickly after the test is over. We largely agree and would argue that in creating assessments that ask students to engage in the skills at the top of the new pyramid (application, creation, analysis, evaluation), instructors can see students' understanding. So, for example, in the Conference Project, the role-playing scenarios, and the roundtables we have discussed throughout this book, we can assess our students' understanding and remembering (the skills lower on the new pyramid) of our course information and concepts by seeing the work they produce in each of those assignments. Of course, varying your use of these kinds of assessment and being very methodical in your evaluation of them is essential (more on that in a minute). A student who can present beautifully may not be as adept at written explanations and should be assessed in both ways, as should a student who writes brilliantly but struggles articulating his or her understandings and analysis verbally. In using formative assessments (which are deeply connected to performance-based assessments) to get at our students' summative understanding of the content, we believe we get to see their mastery of both content and skills because students are empowered and required to perform well at all levels of the pyramid throughout the entirety of the course and in ways that are far deeper than any multiple-choice or essay test we could devise.

The argument that American students needed to emerge from their education with skills and aptitudes that enabled them to utilize their knowledge more effectively drove the shift in pedagogical thinking, then was reaffirmed by the changing nature of knowledge itself. With the Internet, where students can access information in a nanosecond, the memorization of vast amounts of facts seemed to many educators to no longer be the best use of formal, generalist education. And so the focus in many educational settings has now turned toward asking how we teachers can build education to reflect the new normal of a world where skills are as important as knowledge. While traditional testing of knowledge still has its place, we believe that our challenge is to create assessments and assignments that ask students to demonstrate mastery in applying, analyzing, evaluating, and creating. The question is, how can we do that?

To set students up for success in performance-based assessments throughout the term we scaffold lessons and assignments that purposefully ask students to practice skills; then we offer more formal assessments that mimic those assignments. The more formal assessments allow us to evaluate student improvement and mastery of the skills.[4] Utilizing rubrics is especially helpful so that the expectations for mastery are communicated early and often and so that there is a common language with which to discuss progress and success. Like so much in education, support for rubrics waxes and wanes. Skeptics of assessment are usually *really* skeptical about rubrics. But some of that skepticism may stem from a misunderstanding of what rubrics really are. Let's start with what they are not. Rubrics are *not* checklists of requirements that can be quantitatively counted. How many sources must be used, minimum page length for an essay, number of slides or time for a presentation — are all requirements that are quantitative. Transparency about these types of requirements can and should be communicated to students and can be used in the evaluation of student work, but rubrics, when used well, are not quite so objective.

In many ways rubrics are physical representations of the subjective nature of assessment. They communicate with students the spectrum of performance by using words such as *mastering*, *emerging*, and *developing* in a matrix of categories, thereby revealing a variety of possibilities for assessing student work. Suddenly an A is not just an A; it is a judgment that takes into consideration both the strengths and the weaknesses of a particular piece of student work. Rubrics also give permanent expression to what we teachers believe to be the pinnacle of excellence. An instructor can do rubric development beforehand or work with students to create the rubrics. I often use rubrics for the ongoing assessment of individual skills (collaboration, creativity, critical thinking). I create these rubrics in concert with the students and use them throughout the term. Students utilize the rubrics they have helped create to assess themselves (and sometimes even their peers). The specific skill categories then become the basis for the rubric used in the final skill-based assessment (usually a project) at the end of the term.

Assessing true historical skills — argument, judgment, empathy — is not for the faint of heart. These kinds of assessments cannot be approached as if they were midterm or final exams. Cumulative tests are often summative, catchall assessments that figure prominently in the student's grade but come only twice in a term, with little intermediate demonstration of learning. Performance-based assessments require more intentional and more frequent attention to student progress. Rubrics, as instructional tools, offer powerful opportunities to engage in conversation with students about their learning *while* they are learning.

The skills we listed earlier are examples of those we emphasize. Perhaps you have different skills that you believe are valuable for a student of history to learn (being able to engage in a historiographic debate comes to mind). Any skill can be assessed using performance-based tasks and common tools (that is, rubrics). These tasks can be one class period in length or long-term projects. There are strategies for performance-based assessments, but if one connects those strategies with the course, unit, and lesson objectives, then the assessments will meaningfully build students' achievement of skills performance and content learning. We have discussed in-class performance-based assessments throughout this primer in articulating ideas for assignments and projects. The two do not have to (nor, in our opinion, should they necessarily) be different from assessments. To give the assignments the weight of assessments in the minds of students, one can make the assignments count for various amounts of the term grade (5 percent for a role-play, 5 percent for a debate, 15 percent for roundtable discussions, 20 percent for a project, etc.).

Take, for example, a role-play essay or in-class debate. Asking students to read primary sources and then take on the role of the author of that source in a performance gets them to demonstrate their empathetic understanding of a particular source and perspective. If your class size prohibits actual role-play, ask students to write creative essays that represent a particular historical actor's perspective on an issue that does not appear in the source you've assigned. This assignment can occur a couple of times during a semester and can appear as a section on a midterm or final exam via source evaluation. The most important way to make this assignment into an assessment of learning and critical thinking as well as of source evaluation is to make the role-play count as a test, replete with a rubric that explains how students will be evaluated for their demonstration of learning. Doing this several times can help you and your students document their progress in learning. We have found that one of the great rewards of doing assessment in this way is consistent and continual increased student engagement. And don't we all dream of increasing our students' engagement? After all, the more engaged students are, the easier and more rewarding our jobs become.

In short, traditional testing asks students to prove, however briefly, that they know content. In a performance-based classroom, that requisite of knowledge acquisition is added and students are asked, "Can you use it?" As K. Hibbard writes, "When the goal of teaching and learning is *both* knowing and using, then the performance-based classroom emerges."[5] Performance-based assessment, then, actually extends traditional testing as it asks students to apply their content learning to create something new (at least new to them). Increasingly educators are applying developments in and insights from neuroscience to education. One of neuroscience's most well-supported conclusions about learning is that we learn better when learning has personal relevance and emotional importance in our lives and when there are opportunities for repetition.[6] One-shot tests (even three or four per semester) often fail to meet either of these criteria. Project-based learning, however, offers students the opportunity to show what they know and practice what they can do.

As we have alluded to throughout this book, project-based learning is perhaps one of the most important educational innovations of the early twenty-first century, with historical roots in the early twentieth century. It offers an excellent method for encouraging both repetitious content mastery and emotional relevancy to students' lives. It provides an extended performance-based assessment method, which, when conceptualized well, asks students to apply their learning to real-world situations by analyzing, evaluating, and solving problems and creating products to demonstrate all of those skills. As a result, project-based learning is a generative assessment. Students work on an open-ended project to solve a problem or to reimagine reality. In this type of assessment we teachers get to evaluate students' *use* of history rather than simply their knowledge of it.

As we suggested at the outset of this book, our primary objective is to get students to think about what environmental history means for us as humans in the present and future by using the past. We expect our students to create that meaning, which requires that they transcend knowledge acquisition. But in our opinion, the primary purpose of teaching history is to give students material and skills to take with them as they venture into future intellectual and practical challenges. In short, our most important objective for teaching environmental history is that students will be inspired to live a life of inquiry around what it means to be human and to interact with the nonhuman world. When done well, project-based learning has students perform: it can ask students to represent their place through an interactive museum exhibit; it can ask them to assess the soundness of approving Keystone XL and come up with a better idea; it may ask them to apply their learning about resource scarcity to a current dilemma (perhaps water shortages in the U.S. West) and come up with realistic solutions. The best project-based learning requires students to do deep research, reach a sophisticated understanding of the topic at hand, apply impressive creativity, and make meaningful contributions to our collective knowledge.[7]

Another classic historical skill, writing, can be conceptualized anew through the lens of assessment. Many historians think of their writing assignments as helping students to effectively communicate and explain complex historical events. Designing an assessment to have students display this skill can be difficult. Formative writing transcends traditional testing methods of multiple choice or short-answer questions by allowing students an opportunity to apply what they know to new situations. When a writing assignment is creative enough, it requires students to scan their memories, apply their knowledge, and evaluate different perspectives, all in the formulation of an idea unique to them. Writing provides a way for students to think through new ideas rather than just reassuring them that they "got" the information. Explaining to students that they are consultants for an environmental management firm and they have been tasked with contextualizing, corroborating, and sourcing a policy proposal for clean energy requires that they employ historical thinking. After closely reading sources, they must evaluate and combine the information to form a narrative picture. A rubric can help guide them. Such an assignment uses writing to combine inquiry and communication; thus it can also be thought of as a performance-based assessment.

In all likelihood you are thinking, But I always require that my history students write papers. Of course you do. But have you really considered why, and what you are looking for in these papers? Have you conveyed those goals to your students and structured in smaller forms of writing to support those larger goals? In some very concrete ways, writing is thinking. Words and sentences are the instruments that move students' thoughts into new patterns and ideas. With feedback and guidance, writing, as a form of assessment, can improve student learning outcomes, especially if you make those outcomes transparent to your students. Short, informal writing provides a vehicle for students to react and to organize their thoughts. This might take the form of an in-class prompt that gives them ten minutes to gather their thoughts on a film before we discuss it as a class. Or it might be a summary of an article they read. Structured creative writing, such as the Creature Chronicle (the Animals in History assignment discussed in chapter 4) or analyzing a song about bananas, can benefit from a special rubric to emphasize certain skills. Research-based writing, such as a policy recommendation paper, asks students to not only use the skills of evaluating sources and contextualizing but to move beyond the classroom and imagine the ways their writing can have applicability in the world. By tilting the prism to envision broader kinds of skills assessment, writing assignments can mean more than paper prompts and exam questions.

As we teach the important content of environmental history, we continually ask students to evaluate and reflect on the decisions of past human societies as they have interacted with an unpredictable nonhuman nature. That ability to reflect on the past, especially with regard to crucial decision making over time and in a variety of very messy situations, is essential for creating well-informed global citizens who inhabit a fragile earth. John Dewey suggested that the classroom should mimic the democracy into which students would graduate and live. He argued for relevancy, problem solving, and learning by doing so that students emerged with the skills necessary for life in a new century. As we embark on another new century, one in which humanity itself stands on the precipice of environmental change the likes of which we as a species have never encountered, we will require a new kind of global citizenry: one that is profoundly empathetic and deeply thoughtful, that does not shy away from seeking information and processing ideas, that refuses to shirk the challenges of collaborative problem solving, and that understands what it means to live in concert with other beings. We can cross our fingers and hope our students get those habits of mind or luck into that skill set, or we can structure our class objectives and our tests to ensure that, through our robust teaching of environmental history, they have ample opportunities to practice these skills every chance they get. After all, what gets tested gets taught, and what gets taught gets learned.

―――― *Epilogue* ――――

DESPITE ENVIRONMENTAL history's enormous scope and our enthusiasm for teaching it, this field is flawed. As we listened to the many readers' comments during this process, we became acutely aware that capturing it all in a small book on teaching was a formidable task. The book would reflect not only our own choices but the cumulative choices of the larger field. Like much history, the environmental branch suffers from an unevenness of topics, asynchronicity of time, and incomplete representation of various peoples, geographies, and processes. Many topics skew toward the present and may become distorted by today's perspectives rather than yesterday's choices. Some research remains mired in narrow squabbles or overly generalized so as to add little new understanding.

A lack of consensus over terms and definitions continues to bog down newcomers in semantic muck. Similarly an inexplicably uneasy suspicion toward or ignorance of seemingly similar areas of study—historical geography, political ecology, histories of science, human-environmental systems research—keeps the field disciplinarily restricted and perhaps parochial. Some might lament that environmental history is *too* historical or *too* interdisciplinary and thus unmoored from the past and more rightly named environmental studies for its approaches and objectives. All these critiques live in this book. They have inspired in us hours of spirited debate and reflection. They merit even more dialogue. Perhaps such flaws will inspire you to teach these issues or to build new research around them.

Despite these warts and blemishes, we hope this work shows our passion for the discipline of environmental history in which we see enormous potential and possibility and to which we have devoted our lives. Our deepest hope in completing this project is that you and your students might harness this excitement and that, together, we might come to better understand our many environmental pasts in order to share in an environmental future that is bright and inspiring.

—— *Notes* ——

Introduction

1. University departments as reported to the American Historical Association. Townsend, "The Rise and Decline of History Specializations over the Past 40 Years."
2. Casale, "The 'Environmental Turn.'"
3. Rothman, "Conceptualizing the Real."
4. Casale, "The 'Environmental Turn'"; Grusin, *The Nonhuman Turn*.
5. For a classic introduction to the field see "A Round Table: Environmental History." See also the roundtable convened nearly twenty-five years later, "State of the Field." Isenberg, *The Oxford Handbook of Environmental History*, provides a useful and recent overview with more global topics.
6. Benson, "The Urbanization of the Eastern Gray Squirrel in the United States"; Melosi et al., *Energy Capitals*; Santiago, *Ecology of Oil*.
7. Stroud, "Does Nature Always Matter?"
8. Two classic books for investigating salmon are White, *Organic Machine*, and McEvoy, *The Fisherman's Problem*. See also Wadewitz, "Are Fish Wildlife?"
9. Carolyn Merchant made this point well in *Ecological Revolutions*.
10. Recent examples include Liverman, "Conventions of Climate Change"; Dowsley et al., "Should We Turn the Tent?"; Wallis, "Past and Present, Culture in Progress."
11. Langston, "Gender Transformed."
12. A crucial indicator of the health and breadth of environmental history is the growth of scholarly societies in many regions. For example, the International Consortium of Environmental History Organizations (www.iceho.org) includes among its thirty members the American Society of Environmental History, the European Society of Environmental History, Latin American and Caribbean Environmental History Association (Sociedad Latinoamericana y Caribeña de

Historia Ambiental), Association for East Asian Environmental History, and the Australian and New Zealand Environmental History Network.

One. The Fruit

1. hooks, *Teaching to Transgress.*
2. Pollan, *The Botany of Desire*, xvii.
3. "Food Availability and Consumption."
4. Political ecology studies the relationships among political, economic, and social factors and the effects they have on the nonhuman environment. For an introduction, see Robbins, *Political Ecology.*
5. Merchant, "Gender and Environmental History," 1119. For other engaging texts on women and nature, see Merchant, *Death of Nature*, and Sherry Ortner's classic, "Is Female to Male as Nature Is to Culture?"
6. Soluri, *Banana Cultures.*
7. Norton, *Sacred Gifts, Profane Pleasures.*
8. Warman's book *La historia de un bastardo: Maíz y capitalismo* (1988) was translated and reissued as *Corn and Capitalism: How a Botanical Bastard Grew to Global Dominance.* Great syntheses relying heavily on it are in Mann, *1491*, and Pollan, *Omnivore's Dilemma.*
9. Mann, *1491*, 223.
10. Crosby, "The Demographic Effect of American Crops in Europe," 152.
11. McCann, *Maize and Grace.*
12. Crosby, "The Demographic Effect of American Crops in Europe," 161.
13. For an excellent text that adds a gendered analysis to the globalization of food and the unequal effects of transnational capitalism, see Deborah Barndt, *Women Working the NAFTA Food Chain.*

Two. The Seed

1. "General Land Office Records."
2. Cronon, *Changes in the Land*, vii.
3. Dean, *With Broadax and Firebrand*, 3, 5.
4. Guha, *Unquiet Woods*; Langston, *Forest Dreams, Forest Nightmares*; or Hecht and Cockburn, *Fate of the Forest.*
5. Wildlands and Woodlands, accessed April 28, 2017, http://www.wildlandsandwoodlands.org/; Harvard Forest, accessed April 28, 2017, http://harvardforest.fas.harvard.edu/other-tags/wildlands-woodlands.
6. Fairhead and Leach, *Misreading the African Landscape.* See also Davis, *Resurrecting the Granary of Rome*, on deforestation narratives in north Africa.

NOTES TO CHAPTER THREE

7 There are many good texts to use here; you might consult your favorite anthropologist for more recent works. I've used Mann, *1491*, chapter 6, "Cotton (or Anchovies) and Maize," and Diamond, *Guns, Germs, and Steel*, chapter 5, "History's Haves and Have-Nots," as well as Diamond and Bellwood, "Farmers and Their Languages."

Three. The Hatchet

1 Petersen-Boring, "Sustainability and the Western Civilization Curriculum."
2 Robbins, *Political Ecology*, 12.
3 The period was named by the British meteorologist Hubert Lamb. Brian Fagan's work continues to be synthetic and accessible on this topic, especially for students; see *The Little Ice Age* and *The Great Warming*. For a recent comprehensive environmental history overview, see Brooke, *Climate Change and the Course of Global History*. A useful review is Carey, "Climate and History."
4 Richards, *Unending Frontier*, 72.
5 Eagles, "How Fashion Adapted to Climate Change — in the Little Ice Age."
6 Richards, *Unending Frontier*, 81.
7 Endfield, *Climate and Society in Colonial Mexico*.
8 Skopyk, "Rivers of God, Rivers of Empire."
9 Mikhail, "Ottoman Iceland." You might consider pairing this with Hastrup, "A History of Climate Change."
10 Zilberstein, *A Temperate Empire*.
11 Stokes Brown, *Big History*; Christian, "What Is Big History?," and see his curriculum project on his website.
12 Purdy, "American Natures" and *After Nature*.
13 See Weisiger, *Dreaming of Sheep in Navajo Country*. Dr. Weisiger participated in Michelle's U.S. West class through the Western History Association's scholar in the classroom program in 2013. She led the class in the primary source lesson; it was powerful to watch the students begin to understand the complexity of disaster and range management.
14 Johnson, *Climate and Catastrophe in Cuba and the Atlantic World in the Age of Revolution*; Pérez, *Winds of Change*.
15 Grove, *Green Imperialism*, 3.
16 For the Atlantic concept, see Bolster, *The Mortal Sea*; Norton, *Sacred Gifts, Profane Pleasures*; Carney and Rosmonoff, *In the Shadow of Slavery*. For the Pacific world, see Cushman, *Guano and the Opening of the Pacific World*; Melillo, *Strangers on Familiar Soil*.
17 McNeill, *Something New under the Sun*.

Four. The Llama

1. Gade, "The Andes as a Dairyless Civilization."
2. The "humans versus animals" binary presents semantic as well as cultural challenges; for the ease of the reader, we use *animals* as a term excluding humans in the remainder of the chapter.
3. Weisiger, *Dreaming of Sheep in Navajo Country*; Melville, *A Plague of Sheep*; Coleman, *Vicious*; Walker, *The Lost Wolves of Japan*.
4. Ritvo, "On the Animal Turn." See also the book series "The Animal Turn" from Michigan State University Press, edited by Linda Kalof.
5. Ritvo, "On the Animal Turn," 122.
6. Barnosky et al., "Assessing the Causes of Late Pleistocene Extinctions on the Continents."
7. Donlan, "Re-wilding North America." And see letters to the editor in response.
8. Kolbert, "The Mastodon's Molars," chapter 2 in *The Sixth Extinction*; Quammen, "Rarity unto Death."
9. See especially Crosby, chapter 3, "Old World Plants and Animals in the New World," in *The Columbian Exchange*.
10. Thompson, *Where Do Camels Belong?* A similar evolutionary trajectory for horses is explored in Mitchell, *Horse Nations*.
11. Ritvo, "Going Forth and Multiplying."
12. Norton, "Going to the Birds." Jacobs's *Birders of Africa* is an excellent complement to this article.
13. Richards, "Whales and Walruses in the Northern Oceans," in *Unending Frontier*; Soluri, "On Edge."
14. Darnton, "Workers Revolt: The Great Cat Massacre of the Rue Sant-Séverin," chapter 2 in *The Great Cat Massacre and Other Episodes in French Cultural History*; Jacobs, "The Great Bophuthatswana Donkey Massacre"; Kosek, "Ecologies of Empire"; Russell, "'Speaking of Annihilation.'"
15. Derby, "Trujillo, the Goat."
16. Werner, *Smokey the Bear*; "History of Smokey Bear."
17. Kosek, *Understories*, especially chapter 5, "Smokey Bear Is a White Racist Pig."
18. Lewis, "Smokey Bear in Vietnam."
19. Nance, "The Privatization of Animal Life and the Future of Circus Elephants in America."
20. Walker, "Meiji Modernization, Scientific Agriculture, and the Destruction of Japan's Hokkaido Wolf"; Coleman, "Introduction," "Annihilation and Enlightenment," and "Reintroduction," in *Vicious*.
21. Most of the descriptive content is taken from Linnell et al., "Framing the Re-

lationship between People and Nature in the Context of European Conservation."
22 I encourage but don't require them to use their Long Assignment animal, building in some free choice but also demonstrating how the tendency to switch topics repeatedly creates more work for them. This is one way that design works to support your teaching and also to show students the benefits of long-range planning and careful decision making.

Five. The Fields

1 For an engaging personal reflection on working in conservation, see Leal, "Conservation Memories."
2 Cushman, "The Most Valuable Birds in the World"; Wintersteen, "Fishing for Food and Fodder."
3 The classic view is Pratt, *Imperial Eyes*. A more teachable text is Stepan, *Picturing Tropical Nature*.
4 My animals course has taken field trips to the zoo. Excellent contextual reading includes Hanson, *Animal Attractions*, and Horta Duarte, "Zoos in Latin America."
5 Carson, *Silent Spring*, 3.
6 For the use of gender especially in political cartoons, see Hazlett, "'Woman vs. Man vs. Bugs.'"
7 For a recent example critiquing the lack of social context in some scientific fields, see Carey et al., "Glaciers, Gender, and Science," and the immediate and vicious online criticism. That such controversy ensued indicates it hit a nerve.
8 I have used both the entire book and the shorter but still compelling article-length version, Davis, "The Political Ecology of Famine."

Six. The Land

1 Cairncross, "The Death of Distance."
2 United Nations Population Division of the Department of Economic and Social Affairs, "World Urbanization Prospects."
3 "Social Media Fact Sheet."
4 McGonigal, "We Spend 3 Billion Hours a Week as a Planet Playing Videogames."
5 Lewis, "'This Class Will Write a Book'"; Reinhardt, "Finding a Sense of Place."
6 National Institutes of Health, "Exposure of the American People to Iodine-131 from Nevada Nuclear-Bomb Tests."
7 Price, "Thirteen Ways of Seeing Nature in LA."

8. Allen, "A Sense of Place from Space"; Halverson, "The Five Senses of Place."
9. Dreyer, *Zheng He*.
10. Carvajal's personal journal of the 1541–42 expedition was published and edited by the Chilean scholar José Toribio Medina in 1894. The English translation from which you can pull an extract is available in Toribio Medina et al., *The Discovery of the Amazon according to the Account of Friar Gaspar de Carvajal and Other Documents*.
11. Cole, *In the Early Days along the Overland Trail in Nebraska Territory*.
12. Thoreau, "Walking."
13. Two excellent sources for wrapping one's head around the vastness of sense of place are Hayden, *The Power of Place*, and Gieseking et al., *The People, Place and Space Reader*. I do not always assign excerpts of these sources, but they are excellent for informing lectures.
14. Many of Powell's accounts were written after the expedition and thus, depending on the time you have, may be used to delve into the craft of writing history and the importance of archival comparisons among sources. When paired with Martin J. Anderson's "John Wesley Powell's *Explorations of the Colorado River* . . . ," the topic can generate wonderful debate on the truth of history and the meaning of myth-making.
15. Bravo and DeMoor, "The Commons in Europe."
16. An excellent monograph for consultation is Righter, *The Battle over Hetch Hetchy*.
17. Kelman, *A Misplaced Massacre*, 20.
18. Cho, "Hiroshima Peace Memorial Park and the Making of Japanese Postwar Architecture."
19. For this exercise oral histories can be found online about each event. There are also interesting connections between the cranes made in the 1950s by Sadako Sasaki, a young girl who died from leukemia she suffered after experiencing the atomic blast, and the cranes that appear at the 9/11 Memorial. Students often discover these connections in their research and are quite moved by them. See Beser, "How Paper Cranes Became a Symbol of Healing in Japan." See also the official site for the September 11 Memorial and Museum, https://www.911memorial.org/.
20. Vardi, "Imagining the Harvest in Early Modern Europe."
21. To access the work of, as well as excellent background information on, the Hudson River School artists, there is nowhere better than the online exhibits at the Metropolitan Museum of Art: Avery, "The Hudson River School." Images of U.S. agricultural technology, especially advertisements, are widely available on the web. For example, see "McCormick-International Harvester Collection" and Drache, "The Impact of John Deere's Plow."

Seven. The Power

1. Vincent, "Like Butte, a Lonely Dog Hangs On."
2. "Statue of Auditor, the Strip Mine Dog."
3. Ben Guarino, "Thousands of Montana Snow Geese Die after Landing in Toxic, Acidic Mine Pit," *Washington Post*, December 7, 2016; Adams, "1995: Did Toxic Stew Cook the Goose?"
4. Cruikshank, *Do Glaciers Listen?*
5. As many will recognize, this assignment's title is a play on Aldo Leopold's famous essay "Thinking Like a Mountain." Depending on the level of learners you have in your class, you could have them read Leopold's famous treatise and then debate the benefits and drawbacks of anthropomorphizing nonhuman nature.
6. Pritchard, *Confluence*.
7. Worster, *Rivers of Empire*; Wittfogel, *Oriental Despotism*. If you are teaching upper-division college students, this lesson can also serve as an opportunity to delve into issues of historiography and the shifting of the discipline from the 1960s to the 1990s. See also Reisner, *Cadillac Desert*.
8. McNeill and Engelke, *The Great Acceleration*, 34.
9. McNeill, *Something New under the Sun*; McNeill and Engelke, *The Great Acceleration*.
10. "Energy and Water Use."
11. Harris, "Israel Bringing Its Years of Desalination Experience to California."
12. Yergin's book *The Prize: The Epic Quest for Oil, Money and Power* was made into a film by the same name and produced by PBS and BBC in 1992.
13. Scharff, *Taking the Wheel*; Sellers, *Crabgrass Crucible*.
14. See, for instance, the course "Oil and Water: The Gulf Oil Spill of 2010," discussed in Gilmer, "Coursing through the Spill."
15. The literature on climate change is vast, but good histories of it are rare. In addition to the sources mentioned in chapter 3, see Christanson, *Greenhouse*; Ruddiman, *Plows, Plagues, and Petroleum*. Ruddiman's book is provocative because it argues that human influence on climate began long before the industrial revolutions. The advent of agriculture may have played as big a role as the use of fossil fuels. Ruddiman's book could be assigned in a global history course as one of the primary texts, thus adding environment as a central, riveting thread in the course. An interesting account of the intellectual and scientific discovery of climate change is Weart's, *The Discovery of Climate Change*.
16. Wu, "Consumptive Water Use in the Production of Ethanol and Petroleum Gasoline."

17 Findlay, *The Atomic West*. For a compelling connection to health, see Clark, *Radium Girls*.
18 Brown, *Plutopia*.
19 We count in the term *industrialization* dams, outlets for mining waste, sources of cooling, modes of transportation, and more.
20 "Statue of Auditor, the Strip Mine Dog" describes a statue, copper of course, that was built for display at Berkeley Pit viewing stand.

Eight. The People

1 Robert Burns went to prison for five years; his sons received probation. Robert Ward was found not guilty but liable and ordered to pay damages to the Environmental Protection Agency and the state of North Carolina. Details from this recounting can be found in McGurty, "From NIMBY to Civil Rights." See also Bullard, *Dumping in Dixie*. Much additional material on environmental justice comes out of the field of political ecology.
2 Martínez-Alier, "Ecology and the Poor"; Guha, "Radical American Environmentalism and Wilderness Preservation."
3 Peet and Watts, "Liberation Ecology."
4 Sturgeon, *Environmentalism in Popular Culture*.
5 Wakild, "Environmental Justice, Environmentalism, and Environmental History in Twentieth-Century Latin America."
6 Nixon, *Slow Violence and the Environmentalism of the Poor*, 2.
7 For an earlier case study that can be added here, see Myrna Santiago's book *Ecology of Oil*, which looks at the first oil drilling in a tropical country, Mexico in 1900–1938.
8 Saro-Wiwa, *A Month and a Day* and *Genocide in Nigeria*.
9 Nixon, *Slow Violence*, 107; Watts, *The Curse of the Black Gold*.
10 Nixon, *Slow Violence*, 113–15.
11 Okome, *Before I Am Hanged*.
12 Saro-Wiwa, *A Month and a Day*, 2–4, 39–79, 93–122, 147–57.
13 Rather than primary sources, some ethnographic sources that might work for a similar exercise include Auyero and Swistun's ethnographic analysis of an industrial shantytown in Argentina, *Flammable*, and Tsing, *Friction*. Two incredible resources for determining what cases you'd like to teach are the websites of Environmental Justice Organisations, Liabilities, and Trade (www.ejolt.org) and Environmental Justice Atlas (www.ejatlas.org), which profile organizations and issues worldwide. On the atlas you can sort for categories (nuclear, mineral, water, etc.), regions, and featured issues.

14 I've used excerpts from Chevron's "2011 Annual Report," 49–51, and Amazon Watch et al.'s "The True Cost of Chevron."
15 Quote from Suzanne Goldenberg, "Climate Change: The Poor Will Suffer Most," *Guardian*, March 30, 2014, http://www.theguardian.com/environment/2014/mar/31/climate-change-poor-suffer-most-un-report. See also "Synthesis of the 5th IPCC Report on Climate Change," which explains the findings of the IPCC Fifth Assessment Report. That report was produced by over eight hundred scientists and is the most comprehensive global assessment of climate change ever undertaken.
16 For example, if your class allows you time to draw upon some of the early modern examples we discussed in chapter 4 (Zilberstein on early America, Mikhail on Egypt), it might be appropriate to link this discussion to a consideration of change over time.
17 "The Principles of Environmental Justice," adopted 1991, http://www.ejnet.org/ej/principles.pdf. I sometimes organize the project summit around these principles.
18 Dewey, *Democracy and Education*, quote in chapter 12, "Thinking in Education."
19 The Buck Institute has played a key part in ensuring that the number of adherents of project-based learning continues to grow in the twenty-first century. See their website, http://bie.org/, accessed April 28, 2017.
20 As you plan, it is important to remember that you might have to provide source material for the historical examples if there is a dearth of information on the web, as there might be for some locales. The more famous environmental justice events in the United States are easily found (Three Mile Island comes to mind), but if you hope to reveal more obscure events, you may have to provide research materials and use the Environmental Justice Atlas (www.ejatlas.org).

Nine. The Tools

1 In Haraway, *Simians, Cyborgs, and Women*.
2 Cocotas, "Chart of the Day."
3 "If You Printed Off All of the Instagram Photos."
4 Gunderman, "Is the Lecture Dead?" Reese, "Lectures Didn't Work in 1350—and They Still Don't."
5 Increasingly primary documents are being digitized, so our access to more diverse sources is growing daily. Now students can *do* history by accessing these documents and writing about them. In addition to her intriguing work that

helps us think about what makes something "natural," Dolly Jorgensen, a professor at Luleå University of Technology, is an excellent person to follow on Twitter to learn about new digitization of manuscripts the world over. See @DollyJorgensen and her essay "Not by Human Hands."

6 For some of the best printed resources on digital teaching in the classroom, see Kelly et al., *Teaching the Digital Generation*; Fullen, *Stratosphere*. Because the field changes so rapidly, we find the best way to stay up to date is by relying on some of the best educational technology blogs. Two that we use routinely are "Technology Integration" on *Edutopia*, and Martin, *21k12*.

Ten. The Test

1 Hyde, "Five Reasons History Professors Suck at Assessment."
2 Armstrong, "Bloom's Taxonomy." See also Krathwohl and Bloom, *Taxonomy of Educational Objectives*.
3 For a terrific visual representation of this version of Bloom's taxonomy, see Singer, "38 Question Starters Based on Bloom's Taxonomy." I hand it out to my students at the beginning of each semester and use the terms in every rubric so the students can see how each assignment asks them to practice the objectives that are based on this visual representation of learning.
4 The term *skill-based* is often used interchangeably with *performance-based*.
5 Hibbard et al., "What Is Performance-Based Learning and Assessment, and Why Is It Important?"
6 Brown, *Make It Stick*; Jensen, *Teaching with the Brain in Mind*; Medina, *Brain Rules*; Sousa, *How the Brain Learns*.
7 For excellent resources on what the Buck Institute calls "gold standard" project-based learning, see Larmer, *Setting the Standard for Project Based Learning*. See also the Buck Institute website, http://bie.org/. Some teachers worry that there is a profound disconnect between problem-based learning and project-based learning. The two are of the same coin in many ways and can be blended together to make rigorous and rich assessment experiences for students. An excellent article on the distinctions between the two is Larmer's "Project-Based Learning vs. Problem-Based Learning vs. X-BL."

―― *Bibliography* ――

Adams, Duncan. "1995: Did Toxic Stew Cook the Goose?" *High Country News*, December 11, 1995. http://www.hcn.org/issues/49/1520.
Allen, Joseph P. "A Sense of Place from Space: Joseph P. Allen at TEDx Sonoma County." *YouTube*, June 20, 2012. https://www.youtube.com/watch?v=mTM5dpzZOSQ.
Amazon Watch, et al. "The True Cost of Chevron: An Alternative Annual Report." May 2011. http://truecostofchevron.com/2011-alternative-annual-report.pdf.
Anderson, Martin J. "John Wesley Powell's *Explorations of the Colorado River* . . . : Fact, Fiction, or Fantasy?" *Journal of Arizona History* 24, no. 4 (1983): 363–80.
Armstrong, Patricia. "Bloom's Taxonomy." Center for Teaching, Vanderbilt University. Accessed December 16, 2015. https://cft.vanderbilt.edu/guides-sub-pages/blooms-taxonomy/#why.
Auyero, Javier, and Debora Alejandra Swistun. *Flammable: Environmental Suffering in an Argentine Shantytown*. New York: Oxford University Press, 2009.
Avery, Kevin J. "The Hudson River School." In *Heilbrunn Timeline of History*. Metropolitan Museum of Art, October 2004. http://www.metmuseum.org/toah/hd/hurs/hd_hurs.htm.
Barnosky, A. D., Paul L. Koch, Robert S. Feranec, Scott L. Wing, and Alan B. Shabel. "Assessing the Causes of Late Pleistocene Extinctions on the Continents." *Science* 306, no. 5693 (2004): 70–75.
Benson, Etienne. "The Urbanization of the Eastern Gray Squirrel in the United States." *Journal of American History* 100, no. 3 (2013): 691–711.
Beser, Ari. "How Paper Cranes Became a Symbol of Healing in Japan." *National Geographic Voices*, August 28, 2015. http://voices.nationalgeographic.com/2015/08/28/how-paper-cranes-became-a-symbol-of-healing-in-japan/.
Bodanzky, Jorge, and Orlando Senna, dirs. *Iracema: Uma Transa Amazonica*. Bretz Films, 1974.

Bolster, W. Jeffrey. *The Mortal Sea: Fishing the Atlantic in the Age of Sail.* Boston: Belknap Press, 2014.

Bravo, G., and T. DeMoor. "The Commons in Europe: From Past to Future." *International Journal of the Commons* 2, no. 2 (2008): 155–61.

Brooke, John L. *Climate Change and the Course of Global History: A Rough Journey.* Cambridge: Cambridge University Press, 2014.

Brown, Kate. *Plutopia: Nuclear Families, Atomic Cities, and the Great Soviet and American Plutonium Disasters.* Oxford: Oxford University Press, 2013.

Brown, Peter. *Make It Stick: The Science of Successful Learning.* Cambridge, MA: Belknap Press, 2014.

Bullard, Robert D. *Dumping in Dixie: Race, Class, and Environmental Quality.* 3rd ed. Boulder, CO: Westview Press, 2000.

Cairncross, Frances. "The Death of Distance." *Economist*, September 30, 1995.

Carey, Mark. "Climate and History: A Critical Review of Historical Climatology and Climate Change Historiography." *WIREs Climate Change* 3, no. 3 (2012): 233–49.

Carey, Mark, M. Jackson, Alessandro Antonello, and Jaclyn Rushing. "Glaciers, Gender, and Science: A Feminist Glaciology Framework for Global Environmental Change Research." *Progress in Human Geography* 40, no. 6 (2016): 770–93.

Carney, Judith, and Richard Nicholas Rosmonoff. *In the Shadow of Slavery: Africa's Botanical Legacy in the Atlantic World.* Berkeley: University of California Press, 2010.

Carson, Rachel. *Silent Spring.* New York: Houghton Mifflin, 1962.

Casale, Giancarlo. "The 'Environmental Turn': A Teaching Perspective." *International Journal of Middle East Studies* 42, no. 4 (2010): 669–71.

Chevron. "2011 Annual Report." Accessed July 20, 2017. http://www.nioclibrary.ir/free-e-resources/Cheveron%20Texaco/Chevron2011AnnualReport_full.pdf.

Cho, Hyunjung. "Hiroshima Peace Memorial Park and the Making of Japanese Postwar Architecture." *Journal of Architectural Education* 66, no. 1 (2012): 72–83.

Christanson, Gale. *Greenhouse: The 200-Year Story of Global Warming.* New York: Walker, 1999.

Christian, David. "What Is Big History?" *Big History Project.* Accessed September 21, 2017. https://www.bighistoryproject.com/home.

Clark, Claudia. *Radium Girls: Women and Industrial Health Reform, 1910–1935.* Chapel Hill: University of North Carolina Press, 1997.

Cocotas, Alex. "Chart of the Day: Kids Send a Mind Boggling Number of Texts Every Month." *Business Insider*, March 22, 2013. http://www.businessinsider.com/chart-of-the-day-number-of-texts-sent-2013-3.

Cole, Gilbert. *In the Early Days along the Overland Trail in Nebraska Territory, in 1852*. Project Gutenberg. Accessed June 16, 2016. http://www.gutenberg.org/files/31384/31384-h/31384-h.htm.

Coleman, Jon T. *Vicious: Wolves and Men in America*. New Haven, CT: Yale University Press, 2004.

Cronon, William. *Changes in the Land: Indians, Colonists, and the Ecology of New England*. New York: Hill and Wang, 1983.

———. "The Trouble with Wilderness; Or, Getting Back to the Wrong Kind of Nature." In *Uncommon Ground: Rethinking the Human Place in Nature*, edited by William Cronon, 69–90. New York: Norton, 1995.

Crosby, Alfred. *The Columbian Exchange*. New York: Greenwood, 1972.

———. "The Demographic Effect of American Crops in Europe." In *Germs, Seeds, and Animals: Studies in Ecological History*, 148–66. New York: M. E. Sharpe, 1994.

Cruikshank, Julie. *Do Glaciers Listen? Local Knowledge, Colonial Encounters, and Social Imagination*. Vancouver: University of British Columbia Press, 2005.

Cushman, Gregory. *Guano and the Opening of the Pacific World*. Cambridge: Cambridge University Press, 2014.

———. "The Most Valuable Birds in the World: International Conservation Science and the Revival of Peru's Guano Industry, 1909–1965." *Environmental History* 10, no. 3 (2005): 477–509.

Darnton, Robert. *The Great Cat Massacre and Other Episodes in French Cultural History*. New York: Vintage, 1984.

Davis, Diana K. *Resurrecting the Granary of Rome: Environmental History and French Colonial Expansion in North Africa*. Athens: Ohio University Press, 2007.

Davis, Mike. *Late Victorian Holocausts: El Niño Famines and the Making of the Third World*. New York: Verso, 2002.

———. "The Political Ecology of Famine: The Origins of the Third World." In *Liberation Ecologies: Environment, Development and Social Movements*, edited by Richard Peet and Michael Watts, 48–66. 2nd ed. London: Routledge, 2004.

Dean, Warren. *With Broadax and Firebrand: The Destruction of the Brazilian Atlantic Forest*. Berkeley: University of California Press, 1995.

Derby, Lauren. "Trujillo, the Goat: Of Beasts, Men, and Politics in the Dominican Republic." In *Centering Animals in Latin American History*, edited by Martha Few and Zeb Tortorici, 302–28. Durham, NC: Duke University Press, 2013.

Dewey, John. *Democracy and Education: An Introduction to the Philosophy of Education*. New York: Macmillan, 1916. Project Gutenberg. http://www.gutenberg.org/files/852/852-h/852-h.htm.

Diamond, Jared. *Guns, Germs, and Steel: The Fates of Human Societies*. New York: Norton, 1997.

Diamond, Jared, and Peter Bellwood. "Farmers and Their Languages: The First Expansions." *Science* 300, no. 5619 (2003): 597–603.

Donlan, C. Josh. "Re-wilding North America." *Nature* 436, no. 18 (2005): 913–14.

Dowsley, Martha, Shari Gearheard, Noor Johnson, and Jocelyn Inksetter. "Should We Turn the Tent? Inuit Women and Climate Change." *Études/Inuit/Studies* 34, no. 1 (2010): 151–65.

Drache, Hiram M. "The Impact of John Deere's Plow." *Illinois History Teacher* 8, no. 1 (2001): 2–13. Accessed December 12, 2016. http://www.lib.niu.edu/2001/iht810102.html.

Dreyer, Edward L. *Zheng He: China and the Oceans in the Early Ming Dynasty.* New York: Pearson Longman, 2007.

Eagles, Lane. "How Fashion Adapted to Climate Change — in the Little Ice Age." *The Conversation*, September 7, 2017. https://theconversation.com/how-fashion-adapted-to-climate-change-in-the-little-ice-age-82104.

Elvin, Mark. *The Retreat of the Elephants: An Environmental History of China.* New Haven, CT: Yale University Press, 2006.

Endfield, Georgina. *Climate and Society in Colonial Mexico.* Malden, MA: Blackwell, 2008.

"Energy and Water Use." Union of Concerned Scientists. Accessed July 20, 2017. http://www.ucsusa.org/clean-energy/energy-water-use#.WXEb3ojytPY.

Evenden, Matthew. "Reflections: Environmental History Pedagogy beyond History and on the Web." *Environmental History* 14, no. 4 (2009): 737–43.

Fagan, Brian. *The Great Warming: Climate Change and the Rise and Fall of Civilizations.* New York: Bloomsbury, 2008.

———. *The Little Ice Age.* New York: Basic Books, 2000.

Fairhead, James, and Melissa Leach. *Misreading the African Landscape: Society and Ecology in a Forest-Savannah Mosaic.* Cambridge: Cambridge University Press, 1996.

Fernandez-Armesto, Felipe. *The Americas: A Hemispheric History.* New York: Modern Library, 2003.

Findlay, John M. *The Atomic West.* Seattle: University of Washington Press, 1998.

"Food Availability and Consumption." U.S. Department of Agriculture Economic Research Service. Accessed December 12, 2016. https://www.ers.usda.gov/data-products/ag-and-food-statistics-charting-the-essentials/food-availability-and-consumption/.

Fullen, Michael. *Stratosphere: Integrating Technology, Pedagogy and Change Knowledge.* New York: Pearson, 2012.

Gade, Daniel W. "The Andes as a Dairyless Civilization: Llamas and Alpacas as

Unmilked Animals." In *Nature and Culture in the Andes*, 102–17. Madison: University of Wisconsin Press, 1999.

"General Land Office Records." U.S. Department of the Interior, Bureau of Land Management. Accessed April 28, 2017. https://www.glorecords.blm.gov/default.aspx.

Gieseking, Jen Jack, William Mangold, and Cindy Katz, eds. *The People, Place and Space Reader*. New York: Routledge, 2014.

Gilmer, Robert A. "Coursing through the Spill: Notes on Teaching Environmental Justice and Making the Academy Responsive to Contemporary Issues." *Radical History Review* 116 (Spring 2013): 167–89.

Grandin, Temple. "Thinking the Way Animals Do." *Western Horseman*, November 1997, 140–45.

Grove, Richard H. *Green Imperialism: Colonial Expansion, Tropical Island Edens, and the Origins of Environmentalism, 1600–1860*. Cambridge: Cambridge University Press, 1995.

Grusin, Richard, ed. *The Nonhuman Turn*. Minneapolis: University of Minnesota Press, 2015.

Guha, Ramachandra. "Radical American Environmentalism and Wilderness Preservation." *Environmental Ethics* 11, no. 1 (1989): 71–83.

———. *Unquiet Woods: Ecological Change and Peasant Resistance in the Himalaya*. Berkeley: University of California Press, 1990.

Gunderman, Richard. "Is the Lecture Dead?" *Atlantic*, January 29, 2013. http://www.theatlantic.com/health/archive/2013/01/is-the-lecture-dead/272578/.

Halverson, Seré Prince. "The Five Senses of Place: Seré Prince Halverson at TEDx Sonoma County." *YouTube*, June 20, 2012. https://www.youtube.com/watch?v=gadT3B04GJc.

Hanson, Elizabeth. *Animal Attractions: Nature on Display in American Zoos*. Princeton, NJ: Princeton University Press, 2002.

Haraway, Donna. *Simians, Cyborgs, and Women: The Reinvention of Nature*. London: Routledge, 1990.

Harris, Emily. "Israel Bringing Its Years of Desalination Experience to California." *Weekend Edition Sunday*, NPR, June 14, 2015. http://www.npr.org/sections/parallels/2015/06/14/413981435/israel-bringing-its-years-of-desalination-experience-to-california.

Hastrup, Kirsten Blinkenberg. "A History of Climate Change: Inughuit Responses to Changing Ice Conditions in North-West Greenland." *Climatic Change*, February 2016, 1–12.

Hayden, Dolores. *The Power of Place: Urban Landscapes as Public History*. Boston: MIT Press, 1997.

Hazlett, Maril. "'Woman vs. Man vs. Bugs': Gender and Popular Ecology in Early Reactions to *Silent Spring*." *Environmental History* 9, no. 4 (2004): 701–29.

Hecht, Susanna, and Alexander Cockburn. *Fate of the Forest: Developers, Destroyers, and Defenders of the Amazon*. New York: Penguin Books, 1990.

Herzog, Werner, dir. *Aguirre: The Wrath of God*. Werner Herzog Filmproduktion, 1972.

Hibbard, K. Michael, et al. "What Is Performance-Based Learning and Assessment, and Why Is It Important?" In *Teacher's Guide to Performance-Based Learning and Assessment*. ACSD. Accessed January 13, 2016. http://www.ascd.org/publications/books/196021/chapters/What_is_Performance-Based_Learning_and_Assessment,_and_Why_is_it_Important%C2%A2.aspx.

"History of Smokey Bear." *U.S. Forest Service*. Accessed April 28, 2017. http://www.fs.usda.gov/detail/r3/learning/history-culture/?cid=FSBDEV3_021636.

hooks, bell. *Teaching to Transgress: Education as the Practice of Freedom*. New York: Routledge, 1994.

Horta Duarte, Regina. "Zoos in Latin America." *Oxford Research Encyclopedia of Latin American History*. Accessed October 12, 2017. http://latinamericanhistory.oxfordre.com/view/10.1093/acrefore/9780199366439.001.0001/acrefore-9780199366439-e-439.

Hyde, Anne. "Five Reasons History Professors Suck at Assessment." *Journal of American History* 102, no. 4 (2016): 1104–7.

"If You Printed Off All of the Instagram Photos Uploaded in a Year, How Far Would They Reach?" *CEWE Photoworld*. Accessed April 28, 2017. https://cewe-photoworld.com/photos-on-the-web/.

Isenberg, Andrew C. *The Oxford Handbook of Environmental History*. New York: Oxford University Press, 2014.

Jacobs, Nancy J. *Birders of Africa: History of a Network*. New Haven, CT: Yale University Press, 2016.

———. "The Great Bophuthatswana Donkey Massacre: Discourse on the Ass and the Politics of Class and Grass." *American Historical Review* 106, no. 2 (2001): 485–507.

Jensen, Erik. *Teaching with the Brain in Mind*. Alexandria: Association for Supervision and Curriculum Development, 2005.

Johnson, Sherry. *Climate and Catastrophe in Cuba and the Atlantic World in the Age of Revolution*. Chapel Hill: University of North Carolina Press, 2011.

Jorgensen, Dolly. "Not by Human Hands: Five Technological Tenets for Environmental History in the Anthropocene." *Environment and History* 20, no. 4 (2014): 479–89.

Kelly, Frank S., Ted McCain, and Ian Jukes, eds. *Teaching the Digital Generation.* Thousand Oaks, CA: Corwin Press, 2009.

Kelman, Ari. *A Misplaced Massacre: Struggling over the Memory of Sand Creek.* Cambridge, MA: Harvard University Press, 2015.

Kolbert, Elizabeth. *The Sixth Extinction: An Unnatural History.* New York: Picador, 2014.

Kosek, Jake. "Ecologies of Empire: On the New Uses of the Honeybee." *Cultural Anthropology* 25, no. 4 (2010): 650–79.

———. *Understories: The Political Life of Forests in Northern New Mexico.* Durham, NC: Duke University Press, 2006.

Krathwohl, David, and Benjamin Bloom. *Taxonomy of Educational Objectives, Handbook II: Affective Domain (The Classification of Educational Goals).* New York: David McKay, 1956.

Kricher, John. *A Neotropical Companion: An Introduction to the Animals, Plants, and Ecosystems of the New World Tropics.* 2nd ed. Princeton, NJ: Princeton University Press, 1999.

Langston, Nancy. *Forest Dreams, Forest Nightmares: The Paradox of Old Growth in the Inland West.* Seattle: University of Washington Press, 1995.

———. "Gender Transformed: Endocrine Disruptors in the Environment." In *Seeing Nature through Gender*, edited by Virginia J. Scharff, 129–66. Lawrence: University Press of Kansas, 2003.

Larmer, John. "Project-Based Learning vs. Problem-Based Learning vs. X-BL." *Edutopia*, January 6, 2014. http://www.edutopia.org/blog/pbl-vs-pbl-vs-xbl-john-larmer.

———. *Setting the Standard for Project Based Learning: A Proven Approach to Rigorous Classroom Instruction.* Alexandria: Association for Supervision and Curriculum Development, 2015.

Leal, Claudia. "Conservation Memories: Vicissitudes of a Biodiversity Conservation Project in the Rainforests of Colombia, 1992–1998." *Environmental History* 20, no. 3 (2015): 368–95.

Leopold, Aldo. "Thinking Like a Mountain." In *A Sand County Almanac and Sketches Here and There.* New York: Oxford University Press, 1949.

Lewis, James G. "Smokey Bear in Vietnam." *Environmental History* 11, no. 3 (2006): 598–603.

Lewis, Michael. "'This Class Will Write a Book': An Experiment in Environmental History Pedagogy." *Environmental History* 9, no. 4 (2004): 604–19.

Linnell, John D. C., Petra Kaczensky, Ulrich Wotschikowsky, Nicolas Lescureux, and Luigi Boitani. "Framing the Relationship between People and Nature in the Context of European Conservation." *Conservation Biology* 29, no. 4 (2015): 978–85.

Liverman, Diana M. "Conventions of Climate Change: Constructions of Danger and the Dispossession of the Atmosphere." *Journal of Historical Geography* 35, no. 2 (2009): 279–96.

Mann, Charles. *1491: New Revelations of the Americas before Columbus*. New York: Knopf, 2005.

Martin, Jonathan. *21k12* (blog). Accessed December 2016. https://21k12blog.net/.

Martínez-Alier, Joan. "Ecology and the Poor: A Neglected Dimension of Latin American History." *Journal of Latin American Studies* 23, no. 3 (1991): 621–39.

McCann, James. *Maize and Grace: Africa's Encounter with a New World Crop, 1500–2000*. Cambridge, MA: Harvard University Press, 2005.

"McCormick-International Harvester Collection." Wisconsin Historical Society. Accessed December 12, 2016. http://www.wisconsinhistory.org/Content.aspx?dsNav=N:1167.

McEvoy, Arthur. *The Fisherman's Problem: Ecology and Law in the California Fisheries, 1850–1980*. Cambridge: Cambridge University Press, 1990.

McGonigal, Jane. *Reality Is Broken: Why Games Make Us Better and How They Can Change the World*. New York: Penguin, 2011.

———. "We Spend 3 Billion Hours a Week as a Planet Playing Videogames. Is It Worth It? How Could It Be MORE Worth It?" TED. Accessed April 28, 2017. http://www.ted.com/conversations/44/we_spend_3_billion_hours_a_wee.html.

McGurty, Eileen Maura. "From NIMBY to Civil Rights: The Origins of the Environmental Justice Movement." *Environmental History* 2, no. 3 (1997): 301–23.

McNeill, John R. *Something New under the Sun: An Environmental History of the Twentieth Century*. New York: Norton, 2001.

McNeill, John R., and Peter Engelke. *The Great Acceleration: An Environmental History of the Anthropocene since 1945*. Cambridge, MA: Belknap Press, 2014.

Medina, John. *Brain Rules: 12 Principles for Surviving and Thriving at Work, Home, and School*. Seattle: Pear Press, 2014.

Melillo, Edward. *Strangers on Familiar Soil: Rediscovering the Chile-California Connection*. New Haven, CT: Yale University Press, 2015.

Melosi, Martin, Kathleen Brosnan, and Joseph Pratt. *Energy Capitals: Global Influence, Local Impact*. Pittsburgh: University of Pittsburgh Press, 2014.

Melville, Elinor. *A Plague of Sheep: Environmental Consequences of the Conquest of Mexico*. Cambridge: Cambridge University Press, 1997.

Merchant, Carolyn. *The Death of Nature: Women, Ecology, and the Scientific Revolution*. San Francisco: HarperCollins, 1983.

———. *Ecological Revolutions: Nature, Gender and Science in New England.* Chapel Hill: University of North Carolina Press, 1989.

———. "Gender and Environmental History." *Journal of American History* 76, no. 4 (1990): 1117–21.

Mikhail, Alan. "Ottoman Iceland: A Climate History." *Environmental History* 20, no. 2 (2015): 262–84.

Miller, Shawn. *An Environmental History of Latin America.* New York: Cambridge University Press, 2007.

Mitchell, Peter. *Horse Nations: The Worldwide Impact of the Horse on Indigenous Societies Post-1492.* New York: Oxford University Press, 2015.

Mitman, Gregg. "Pachyderm Possibilities: The Media of Science, Politics, and Conservation." In *Thinking with Animals: New Perspectives on Anthropomorphism*, edited by Lorraine Daston and Gregg Mitman, 175–95. New York: Columbia University Press, 2005.

Morrissey, Katherine. *Mental Territories: Mapping the Inland Empire.* Ithaca, NY: Cornell University Press, 1997.

Nance, Susan. "The Privatization of Animal Life and the Future of Circus Elephants in America." *AHA Today*, May 31, 2016. http://blog.historians.org/2016/05/circus-elephants-in-america/.

National Institutes of Health. "Exposure of the American People to Iodine-131 from Nevada Nuclear-Bomb Tests: Review of the National Cancer Institute Report and Public Health Implications." NCBI, 1999. http://www.ncbi.nlm.nih.gov/books/NBK100848/.

Nixon, Rob. *Slow Violence and the Environmentalism of the Poor.* Cambridge, MA: Harvard University Press, 2011.

Norton, Marcy. "Going to the Birds: Animals as Things and Beings in Early Modernity." In *Early Modern Things: Objects and Their Histories, 1500–1800*, edited by Paula Findlen, 53–83. London: Routledge, 2012.

———. *Sacred Gifts, Profane Pleasures: A History of Tobacco and Chocolate in the Atlantic World.* Ithaca, NY: Cornell University Press, 2008.

Okome, Onookome. *Before I Am Hanged: Ken Saro-Wiwa—Literature, Politics, and Dissent.* Trenton, NJ: Africa World Press, 1999.

Ortner, Sherry. "Is Female to Male as Nature Is to Culture?" In *Women, Culture, and Society*, edited by Michelle Zimbalist Rosaldo and Louise Lamphere, 67–88. Stanford, CA: Stanford University Press, 1974.

Orwell, George. "Shooting an Elephant." *New Writing*, 1936.

Peet, Richard, and Michael Watts. "Liberation Ecology: Development, Sustainability, and Environment in an Age of Market Triumphalism." In *Liberation*

Ecologies, edited by Richard Peet and Michael Watts, 1–45. New York: Routledge, 1996.

Pérez, Louis. *Winds of Change: Hurricanes and the Transformation of Nineteenth-Century Cuba*. Chapel Hill: University of North Carolina Press, 2001.

Petersen-Boring, Wendy. "Sustainability and the Western Civilization Curriculum: Reflections on Cross-Pollinating the Humanities and Environmental History." *Environmental History* 15, no. 2 (2010): 288–304.

Pollan, Michael. *The Botany of Desire*. New York: Random House, 2002.

———. *The Omnivore's Dilemma: A Natural History of Four Meals*. New York: Penguin, 2006.

Pratt, Mary Louise. *Imperial Eyes: Travel Writing and Transculturation*. New York: Routledge, 1992.

Price, Jennifer. "Thirteen Ways of Seeing Nature in LA." *Believer* 4, no. 3 (2006). https://www.believermag.com/issues/200604/?read=article_price.

Pritchard, Sara B. *Confluence: The Nature of Technology and the Remaking of the Rhône*. Cambridge, MA: Harvard University Press, 2011.

Purdy, Jedediah. *After Nature*. Cambridge, MA: Harvard University Press, 2015.

———. "American Natures: The Shape of Conflict in Environmental Law." *Harvard Environmental Law Review* 36 (2012): 169–228.

Quammen, David. "Rarity unto Death." In *Song of the Dodo: Island Biogeography in an Age of Extinctions*. New York: Scribner, 1996.

Reese, Hope. "Lectures Didn't Work in 1350 — and They Still Don't: A Conversation with David Thornburg about Designing a Better Classroom." *Atlantic*, November 15, 2013. http://www.theatlantic.com/education/archive/2013/11/lectures-didnt-work-in-1350-and-they-still-dont-work-today/281514/.

Reinhardt, Bob H. "Finding a Sense of Place: A Surprising Experiment in Place-Based Collaborative Learning." *Perspectives on History*, December 2013.

Reisner, Marc. *Cadillac Desert: The American West and Its Disappearing Water*. New York: Penguin Books, 1993.

Richards, John. *Unending Frontier: An Environmental History of the Early Modern World*. Berkeley: University of California Press, 2003.

Righter, Robert. *The Battle over Hetch Hetchy: America's Most Controversial Dam and the Birth of Modern Environmentalism*. New York: Oxford University Press, 2006.

Ritvo, Harriet. "Going Forth and Multiplying: Animal Acclimatization and Invasion." *Environmental History* 17, no. 2 (2012): 404–14.

———. "On the Animal Turn." *Daedalus* 136, no. 4 (2007): 118–22.

Robbins, Paul. *Political Ecology*. Malden, MA: Blackwell, 2004.

Rothman, Hal. "Conceptualizing the Real: Environmental History and American Studies." *American Quarterly* 54, no. 3 (2002): 485–97.

"A Round Table: Environmental History." *Journal of American History* 76, no. 4 (1990): 1087–147.

Ruddiman, William F. *Plows, Plagues, and Petroleum: How Humans Took Control of Climate*. Princeton, NJ: Princeton University Press, 2010.

Russell, Edmund P. "'Speaking of Annihilation': Mobilization for War against Human and Insect Enemies, 1914–1945." *Journal of American History* 82, no. 4 (1996): 1505–29.

Santiago, Myrna. *Ecology of Oil: Environment, Labor, and the Mexican Revolution*. Cambridge: Cambridge University Press, 2006.

Saro-Wiwa, Ken. *Genocide in Nigeria: The Ogoni Tragedy*. Port Harcourt: Saros International, 1992.

———. *A Month and a Day: A Detention Diary*. New York: Penguin Books, 1995.

Scharff, Virginia. *Taking the Wheel: Women and the Coming of the Motor Age*. New York: Free Press, 1991.

Sellers, Christopher. *Crabgrass Crucible: Suburban Nature and the Rise of Environmentalism in Twentieth-Century America*. Chapel Hill: University of North Carolina Press, 2012.

Silverman, Helaine. "Touring Ancient Times: The Past and Presented Past in Contemporary Peru." *American Anthropologist* 104, no. 3 (2002): 881–903.

Singer, Jason. "38 Question Starters Based on Bloom's Taxonomy." *Curriculet*, June 17, 2014. http://blog-temp.curriculet.com/38-question-starters-based-blooms-taxonomy/.

Singer, Peter. *Animal Liberation: A New Ethics for Our Treatment of Animals*. New York: HarperCollins, 1975.

Skopyk, Bradley. "Rivers of God, Rivers of Empire: Climate Extremes, Environmental Transformation and Agroecology in Colonial Mexico." *Environment and History* (forthcoming).

"Social Media Fact Sheet." Pew Research Center, January 12, 2017. http://www.pewinternet.org/fact-sheets/social-networking-fact-sheet/.

Soluri, John. *Banana Cultures: Agriculture, Consumption, and Environmental Change in Honduras and the United States*. Austin: University of Texas Press, 2006.

———. "On Edge: Fur Seals and Hunters along the Patagonian Littoral, 1860–1930." In *Centering Animals in Latin American History*, edited by Martha Few and Zeb Tortorici, 243–69. Durham, NC: Duke University Press, 2013.

Sousa, David. *How the Brain Learns*. Thousand Oaks, CA: Corwin Press, 2011.

Spence, Mark David. *Dispossessing the Wilderness: Indian Removal and the Making of the National Parks*. New York: Oxford University Press, 2000.

"State of the Field: American Environmental History." *Journal of American History* 100, no. 1 (2013): 120–44.

"Statue of Auditor, the Strip Mine Dog." *Roadside America*, October 2006. http://www.roadsideamerica.com/story/12137.

Stepan, Nancy Leys. *Picturing Tropical Nature*. Ithaca, NY: Cornell University Press, 2001.

Stokes Brown, Cynthia. *Big History: From the Big Bang to the Present*. New York: New Press, 2007.

Stroud, Ellen. "Does Nature Always Matter? Following Dirt through History." *History and Theory* 42, no. 4 (2003): 75–81.

Sturgeon, Noel. *Environmentalism in Popular Culture: Gender, Race, Sexuality and the Politics of the Natural*. Tucson: University of Arizona Press, 2009.

"Synthesis of the 5th IPCC Report on Climate Change." IPCC, 2014. https://www.ipcc.ch/report/ar5/syr/.

"Technology Integration." Edutopia. Accessed December 2016. https://www.edutopia.org/technology-integration.

Thompson, Ken. *Where Do Camels Belong? Why Invasive Species Aren't All Bad*. London: Greystone Books, 2014.

Thoreau, Henry David. "Walking." *Atlantic*, June 1862. http://www.theatlantic.com/magazine/archive/1862/06/walking/304674/.

Toribio Medina, José, H. C. Heaton, and Bertram T. Lee, trans. *The Discovery of the Amazon according to the Account of Friar Gaspar de Carvajal and Other Documents*. Whitefish, MT: Kessinger Legacy Reprints, 2010.

Townsend, Robert B. "The Rise and Decline of History Specializations over the Past 40 Years." *Perspectives on History*, December 2015. https://www.historians.org/publications-and-directories/perspectives-on-history/december-2015/the-rise-and-decline-of-history-specializations-over-the-past-40-years.

Tsing, Anna Lowenhaupt. *Friction: An Ethnography of Global Connection*. Princeton, NJ: Princeton University Press, 2005.

Tuan, Yi-Fu. *Topophilia: A Study of Environmental Perceptions, Attitudes and Values*. New York: Columbia University Press, 1990.

United Nations Population Division of the Department of Economic and Social Affairs. "World Urbanization Prospects, the 2014 Revision." United Nations. Accessed April 2017. http://esa.un.org/unpd/wup/.

Vardi, Liana. "Imagining the Harvest in Early Modern Europe." In *Agrarian Studies: Synthetic Work at the Cutting Edge*, edited by James C. Scott, 86–138. New Haven, CT: Yale University Press, 2001.

Vincent, Matt. "Like Butte, a Lonely Dog Hangs On." *High Country News*, December 9, 2002. http://www.hcn.org/issues/240/13599.

Wadewitz, Lissa. "Are Fish Wildlife?" *Environmental History* 16, no. 3 (2011): 423–27.

Wakild, Emily. "Environmental Justice, Environmentalism, and Environmental History in Twentieth-Century Latin America." *History Compass* 11, no. 2 (2013): 163–76.

Walker, Brett. *The Lost Wolves of Japan*. Seattle: University of Washington Press, 2005.

———. "Meiji Modernization, Scientific Agriculture, and the Destruction of Japan's Hokkaido Wolf." *Environmental History* 9, no. 2 (2004): 248–74.

Wallis, Velma. "Past and Present, Culture in Progress." In *Arctic Voices: Resistance at the Tipping Point*, edited by Subhankar Banerjee, 486–98. New York: Seven Stories Press, 2013.

Warman, Arturo. *Corn and Capitalism: How a Botanical Bastard Grew to Global Dominance*. Translated by Nancy L. Westrate. Chapel Hill: University of North Carolina Press, 2003.

Watts, Michael, ed. *The Curse of the Black Gold: Fifty Years of Oil in the Niger Delta*. New York: Powerhouse, 2008.

Weart, Spencer. *The Discovery of Climate Change*. Cambridge, MA: Harvard University Press, 2008.

Weiner, Douglas R. *Models of Nature: Ecology, Conservation, and Cultural Revolution in Soviet Russia*. Pittsburg: University of Pittsburg Press, 2000.

Weisiger, Marsha. *Dreaming of Sheep in Navajo Country*. Seattle: University of Washington Press, 2009.

Werner, Jane. *Smokey the Bear*. Illustrations by Richard Scarry. Racine, WI: Golden Press, 1955.

White, Richard. *Organic Machine: The Remaking of the Columbia River*. New York: Hill and Wang, 1996.

Wintersteen, Kristin. "Fishing for Food and Fodder: The Transnational Environmental History of Humboldt Current Fisheries in Peru and Chile since 1945." PhD diss., Duke University, 2011.

Wittfogel, Karl. *Oriental Despotism: A Comparative Study of Total Power*. New York: Vintage Books, 1981.

Worster, Donald. *Rivers of Empire: Water, Aridity, and the Growth of the American West*. New York: Oxford University Press, 1992.

Wu, M., et al. "Consumptive Water Use in the Production of Ethanol and Petroleum Gasoline." Argonne Lab Report, Energy Systems Division, U.S. Department of Energy Office of Scientific and Technical Information, January

2009. http://www.circleofblue.org/wp-content/uploads/2010/09/Water-Consumption-in-Ehtanol-and-Petroleum-Production.pdf.

Yergin, Daniel. *The Prize: The Epic Quest for Oil, Money, and Power.* New York: Free Press, 1991.

Zilberstein, Anya. *A Temperate Empire: Making Climate Change in Early America.* New York: Oxford University Press, 2016.

Index

active learning, 30
actors (historical), 4, 23, 34, 36, 49, 58, 80, 89, 126–27
Adobe Reader, 134
Africa, 46, 54, 57, 60; East, 91; South, 59; West, 35, 43
African Americans, 93, 115
Africanized bees, 58
Africans, 22, 60, 93
Age of Revolutions, 49
agriculture, 4–5, 15–16, 18–20, 23, 39, 49–50, 103, 173; crop failures, 43
Alaska, 101, 109
Amazon (company), 14
Amazon rain forest, 32, 50, 73–75, 90, 119
Amazon River, 74, 90, 103
American Indians, 87, 89, 91
American South, 16
American West, xii, 100. *See also* U.S. West
analysis, 4, 7–8, 17, 21, 60, 75, 89, 101, 105–6, 117, 129, 138, 142–44
Andes, 22, 73
Angkor Wat, 42
animals, 9, 11, 24, 32, 35, 53–67, 75–76, 89, 92, 103, 132. *See also* wildlife
applied disciplinary objectives, 72

Arapaho, 95
Arctic, 50, 100
Arizona Science Center, 131
Asia, xii, 7, 42, 44, 46, 89, 93, 127; Southeast, 90
assessment, 10, 31, 106, 114, 125, 129, 137–38, 141–49; formative, 31, 144; performance-based, 144–48; project-based, 137
assignments, 3, 10–11, 15, 21, 29–31, 33, 55–56, 63–66, 69, 72, 74, 78–79, 102–3, 106, 111, 122, 136, 143–44, 146, 148–49; Animal Policy Brief, 64; Conference Project, 125–26, 128, 143; Creature Chronicle, 65, 149; entry document, 126; Long Assignment, 63; Three Lenses Approach, 64
astronomy, 80
Atacama Desert, 73
Atlantic Ocean, 22, 49–50, 57
Australia, 57–58

banana, xii, 16–23, 25, 149; Big Mike, 18; Cavendish, 18
Banana Republic (company), 19
Berkeley Pit, 99–100, 111
Beverley, Robert, 89
Big History, 46

INDEX

biodiversity, 7, 72, 106, 118
biology, 7, 36, 63, 72, 76–78
Bloom, Benjamin, 142; Bloom's taxonomy, 143
Boise River, 78
botany, 80
Bradford, William, 89
Brazil, 33, 37, 66, 82
Brockovich, Erin, 128
Bureau of Land Management, 79, 112
Burns, Robert, 115
Bush, George W., 48

California, 108, 128
Cambodia, 37
camels, 43, 53–54, 58
Camino Real, 30
Canada, 24, 37, 50
capitalism, 19, 23–24, 46
Caribbean, 49, 59
Carson, Rachel, 81
Carvajal, Gaspar de, 93
Central Arizona Project, 108
Chaco Canyon, 42
chemistry, 80, 102
Chevron-Texaco Oil Company, 76, 119, 121
Cheyenne (people), 95
Chicago River, 102
children's stories, 29, 60, 64
China, 37, 61, 82, 105; Song, 42
chocolate, 21
civil rights, 116
Civil War, 47, 58
classroom, xi–xii, 3, 9, 11, 14, 25, 34, 39, 41, 49, 69, 72, 74, 77, 79, 86, 88, 93, 101, 113–14, 116–17, 123–24, 131, 134–38, 146, 149
climate, 5, 40–45, 82, 113; climate change, xi, 9, 19, 41, 44–45, 57, 81, 100, 109, 123, 129; climate history, 40–41; climatic events, 82
Cocha Cashu Biological Station, 74
Cofán, 121–22
collaborative setting, 125, 127
collective place, 4
Colombia, 37
colonialism, 49–50, 57, 90, 93
Colorado, ix, 103
Colorado River, ix, 92, 102–3, 110; Colorado River Compact of 1922, 103
Columbia River, 102, 110–11
Congo River, 103
conservation, 50, 62, 72–75, 91, 94–95, 137
consumerism, 18–19
consumptive practices, 100
context, 9, 11, 15, 48, 72, 74, 81–82, 95, 97, 101–2, 116–17, 119
corn, 14–15, 21–23, 25
courses: design of, x, 2, 11, 27, 50, 101, 108, 114, 142; objectives of, 27–30, 79, 125, 129, 136, 142, 146; planning of, 2–3, 10, 45, 77–78
critical thinking, 14, 117, 124–25, 129, 134, 145–46
Cuba, 49
cultural barriers, 25
Cusco, 73, 75
Cuyahoga River, 102
cyborg, 131–33, 135–36, 139

Dakota Access Pipeline, 109–10
deadlines, 127
debate, 1, 3, 19–20, 37, 45, 50, 57, 67, 74–75, 79, 93–95, 100
deforestation, 36
determinism, 5, 23
Dewey, John, 125, 149
digital generation, 132–33

digital learners, 133, 138
digital sandbox, 135
Diné (Navajo), 48
disasters, 47–49
discussion, xi, 2–3, 14–15, 17, 19, 21, 23, 28, 33, 36–37, 51, 56, 58, 61–64, 66, 69, 73, 77, 82, 88, 90–92, 95, 101, 109, 120–24, 126–29, 133–35, 137, 141, 146; roundtable, 9, 36–38, 57, 63, 143, 146
disease, 43, 57, 113
diversity, 9, 35, 96, 114, 124, 127
documentary, 15–16, 75, 108, 119, 121–22
Dolly the sheep, 65
Dominican Republic, 60
drought, 9, 42–43, 49, 82, 104, 123
dualisms, 132–33

ecology, 6, 32, 36, 72, 80, 105; ecological consequences, 6; ecological interdependence, 47; ecological network, 25; political, 19, 40, 151
Economist, 85
ecosystem, 32, 34–35, 37, 91, 100, 102, 106, 108–9
Ecuador, 116, 119, 121–22
EduCreations, 135
Egypt, 39, 42, 44
Elwha Dam, 106
energy, 9, 39–41, 46–47, 69, 99–102, 105–13, 148
environmental history, ix–xii, 1–7, 9–11, 13–20, 25, 27, 29–32, 36, 39–40, 45–46, 50–51, 54, 69, 72, 77–79, 82, 85, 87, 93–96, 99–102, 104–5, 108, 110–11, 113–14, 124, 126, 132, 137, 139, 142, 147, 149, 151–52; environmental historians, xii, 2, 4–5, 7–8, 17, 27, 43–44, 46, 49, 54–55, 64, 76–77, 79–80, 102, 107, 114, 141, 148
environmentalism, 106, 116, 118, 122

environmental justice, 9–10, 95, 100, 116–17, 123–29
environmental perspectives, 9, 27, 36, 50, 116
Environmental Protection Agency, 127
environmental studies, 4, 55, 72, 151
Ethiopia, 22
Eurasia, 53
Europe, 5, 7, 21, 23, 42, 44, 46, 59, 61–62, 93, 97; European encounters, 24, 50; European exploration, 50
Europeans, 6, 22
evaluation, 2, 28–29, 142–43, 145–46
experiential learning, 72
extinction, 55–58, 65
Exxon Valdez, 109

Fajardo, Pablo, 119, 121–22
feminism, 131
field trip, 9, 19, 25, 78, 85; virtual, 86
fieldwork, 77
First National People of Color Environmental Leadership Summit, 124
flipped classroom, 134–35
food, 9, 13–18, 20–23, 25, 40, 53–54, 86, 99–101, 111, 123
Food and Drug Administration, 65
forestry, 80
Forest Service, 60–61
formative writing, 148
France, 22, 37, 59
fruit, 9, 11, 16–18, 20

Genbaku Dome, 96
gender relations, 20
General Land Office, 31
geographic information system (GIS), 31
geography, 5, 7, 34–35, 45, 87, 90, 92–93, 96, 102, 109, 151
geological forces, 1

179

Gilded Age, 18, 95
Glen Canyon, 103
Google, 14, 31, 139; Google Docs, 92, 137–38; Google Earth, 85; Google Maps, 30, 85
Grand Canyon, 92
Great Britain, 120
Great Plains, 24, 44
Ground Zero, 97
Guatemala, 34
Gulf of Mexico, 109

Hannibal, 65
Harvard Forest, 35
hatchet, xii, 9, 11, 39–41, 45, 47, 49–51, 77, 101, 107–8
Hetch Hetchy, 94
high-fructose corn syrup, 21
Hiroshima, 96–97; Hiroshima Peace Memorial Park, 97
historical methods, 3, 7–8, 11
historiography, 2, 32, 54, 118
Hoover Dam, 105
horses, 30, 57, 62, 90, 132
Houston, 48
Hudson River School, 91
human experience, 2, 8, 28, 47. *See also* humanity
humanities, 1, 80–82
humanity, 2, 5–6, 18, 46, 55, 111, 121, 149. *See also* human experience
human story, 4, 41
Humboldt River, 90
hurricanes, 49, 106; Harvey, 123; Irma, 123; Katarina, 47, 123
husbandry, 14, 55, 59
hydrology, 80, 102

Iceland, 42, 44
imperialism, 19, 76, 82

India, 33, 61, 82, 95, 105
industrialization, 19, 23–24, 105, 111
Inka, 22, 73–74
Instagram, 19–20, 86, 132, 137
intellectual history, 93–94
Intergovernmental Panel on Climate Change (IPCC), 123, 126
invasion, 55–58
Israel, 108
Italy, 22, 65

Keystone XL, 109–10, 147

Lago Agrio oil field, 121
Laki volcano, 44
landscape, 7, 14, 20, 29–31, 33, 35–36, 50, 73, 76, 89, 91, 95–96, 98, 110, 112, 117
Latin America, ix–xii, 7, 20, 33, 66, 74–75, 118, 127
learning outcomes, 27, 29, 148
lecture, 134–36
Leopold, Aldo, 75
lesson objectives, 146
lessons, x, xii, 7, 11, 16–17, 24, 45, 49, 65, 78, 81, 88, 97–98, 102–3, 105–7, 109, 144, 146
Little Ice Age, 43
llama, xii, 9, 53–54, 57–58, 63, 67, 101
Los Angeles, 88, 103

Machu Picchu, 75
maize, 21–23. *See also* corn
Manu National Park, 74
Mariátegui, José, 74
Maya, 42
McDonald's, 14
Medieval Warming, 42
Mediterranean, 50
megafauna, 57, 61
memory, 95–97
Mesoamerica, 59

Mesopotamia, 37
Mexico, 21–24, 37, 43, 50, 58, 109
millennials, 132
mini-lecture, 135
Mississippi River, 102
modes of interaction, 55–56, 59–60, 64
modes of production, 20
Montana, 99, 112
Muir, John, 93–94

Narmada River, 105
narrative, 7–9, 29, 40–41, 47–48, 50, 82, 101, 108–10, 113, 119; chronological, 56; declensionist, 5, 33; political, 46; progressive, 5, 33, 44; thematic, 108
National Park Service, 95
nation-state, 6, 39, 46, 50, 97, 105, 127
natural history, 4, 63, 80
natural resources, 94, 101, 111, 118
natural world, 3, 9, 47, 75, 81, 96–97
nature, 4–6, 8–11, 13, 17–20, 22, 25, 28–29, 33–35, 40–41, 46–47, 54–56, 60–61, 63, 72–73, 76–78, 80–81, 88–89, 91, 97–98, 101–2, 105, 108, 111, 124–25, 127, 132, 136, 141, 144–45, 149; classic, 56; harmonious, 6
nature writing, 80
Netflix, 132
Nevada Test Site, 87
New Deal, 48
New England, 22, 32, 35, 89
New Mexico, ix, 30, 60, 110
New Orleans, 48
newspaper articles, 29, 64, 82, 122
New World, 57
New York City, 17, 97
New York Times, 16
Niger Delta, 109, 119–20
Nigeria, 109, 116, 119–20, 122
Nile River, 44, 103

No Child Left Behind, 141
nonhuman environment, 91, 93, 101
nonhuman nature, 5, 20, 29, 33, 54, 127, 149
North America, 42, 44, 50, 57–58, 62
North Carolina, 115, 117

Oak Ridge National Lab, 110
Oceanic History, 50
Ogoni, 119–22
oil, 37, 74, 100, 107–10, 112, 117–19, 121–22
Old World, 22, 57
online learning management system, 134
Oregon, ix, 33, 89
Oregon Trail, 89
Orinoco River, 90, 103
ornithology, 80
Ottoman Empire, 61, 97; Egypt, 44; Iceland, 44

Panama Blight, 17
Panama Disease, 18
pedagogy, x–xi, 2, 14, 37, 132–33, 136, 138–39
perspectival questions, 76
Peru, 37, 63, 72–75
pesticides, 81
Pilgrims, 22
plants, 15, 21, 24, 43, 75–76, 101, 103, 108
Pleistocene, 46, 56–57, 60
plutonium, 110
political cartoons, 81
PollEverywhere, 133
Polo, Marco, 89
Poma, Guaman, 74
Powell, John Wesley, 92–93
power differentials, 34, 125
PowerPoint, 62, 136, 138
preservation, 91, 94–95, 116

INDEX

Prezi, 138
primary document, 73, 76. *See also* sources: primary
prior appropriation, 104
problem-based writing assignments, 136
problem solving, 14, 49, 106, 117, 124–25, 128–29, 137, 149
Progressive Era, 47
project-based learning, 10, 115–16, 124–26, 128–29, 138, 147–48
provisioning, 39, 57, 62
Pueblo, 30

real-world application, 117
Reclamation Act of 1902, 105
Reconstruction, 47
red deer, 61–62
relevance, 14, 16, 18, 21, 23–25, 33, 147
research, 2–4, 16, 18, 20, 22, 43, 56–57, 62–63, 65–66, 74, 76, 81, 95, 97, 99, 102, 107, 111, 117, 123–29, 137–38, 148; historical, 7, 63; research-based writing, 149; research paper, 63; scientific, 61, 74, 80–81
resources, 94–95, 101, 123–24, 126; natural, 94, 101, 111, 118
revision, 128
Revolutionary War, 47
Rhône River, 105
Rillito River, 92
Rio de Janeiro, 33
Rio Grande, 102
Rio Madre de Dios, 75
Rockefeller, J. D., 108
Roosevelt, Teddy, 94
rubrics, 129, 141, 144–46, 148–49

Saguaro National Park, 79
salmon, 4, 65
Sand Creek Massacre, 95–96
Santa Fe Railroad, 30
Saro-Wiwa, Ken, 119–22
Saudi Arabia, 105
scarcity, 43, 98, 104, 126, 148. *See also* shortage
science, 9, 13, 39, 41, 56–57, 69, 72, 76–77, 79–82, 89, 113, 131–32, 147, 151
scientific articles, 56–57, 74–79
scientific field guides, 29, 75
seed, xii, 9, 11, 22, 25, 27, 30, 33–36, 38, 77
sense of place, xii, 30, 69, 85, 87–93, 95
sheep, 5–6, 48, 54, 65
Shell Oil Company, 119–20
shortage, 17, 101, 104, 106, 148. *See also* scarcity
Skype, 126
slow violence, 118–19, 121–22, 129
SmartBoard, 136
Smokey Bear, 56, 60
Snapchat, 86, 132
social media, 19–20, 136
sources, 7–8, 15–16, 28–29, 36, 63–64, 82, 88, 90–91, 94–96, 124, 128, 134, 137, 144, 148–49; primary, 3, 16, 48, 89, 91, 93, 110, 146; reliability of, 28; secondary, 66, 91, 97, 134
South Africa, 59
South America, 53
Soviet Union, 110
standards, 141–42
St. Louis, 48
student achievement, 125, 142
student learning, 10, 28–29, 142, 148
supply and demand, 18
Survey Monkey, 138
Switzerland, 43
syllabus, xii, 2, 11, 28–29, 36–37, 45, 51, 56, 100–101, 108
synthesis, 142

INDEX

Tanzania, 37
teaching: mechanics of, 2; strategies for, xi–xii, 3, 8, 38, 41, 48–49, 61, 69, 116, 145–46; team, 77
technology, 9–10, 46, 79–81, 98, 105, 109, 114, 131–33, 135–39; communication, 85, 132, 135, 137; computer, 136; digital, 85–86
TED Talks, 88
tests, 10, 143–47, 149
Timbuktu, 43
timelines, 9, 16, 39–40, 45–47, 55, 101, 107, 121
tobacco, 21
topophilia, 93
Trujillo, Rafael, 60
Tucson, x, 79, 92, 103, 126, 137–38
Tumblr, 132
Twitter, 20, 114, 133–34, 137

United Fruit Company (UFC), 18, 20
United Nations, 123, 126
United States, xi–xii, 16, 18, 24, 31, 50, 53, 58, 61, 65, 79, 86, 92–93, 95, 105–6, 110, 116, 120, 127, 141
universal values, 5
U.S. Department of Agriculture, 16
U.S. History, x, 18, 47–48, 88, 101, 126
U.S. West, ix, 7, 35, 37, 44–45, 60, 92, 102, 107, 110, 112, 148; Intermountain West, ix, 89. *See also* American West
Ute Indians, 92

VoiceThread, 135

Wall Street, 74
Ward, Robert, 115
Ward Transformer Company, 116
Warren County, 115–17
water, ix, 6, 9, 14, 43, 78, 94, 97, 99–113, 116, 119, 121, 126–29, 132, 137–38, 148; water rights, 104
weather, 41, 43, 86, 109, 123, 129, 131; extreme patterns of, 49
Western Hemisphere, 21, 50
Westminster Kennel Club Dog Show, 61
westward expansion, 47
wheat, 21–22, 24–25
Wikispace, 137
wilderness, 89, 91, 94, 100, 116
wildlife, 6, 47, 57, 116. *See also* animals
Winnie the Pooh, 63
wolves, 54, 61
World War I, 24, 44
World War II, 96, 107, 109
Wyoming, 103

Yangtze River, 103
Yellow River, 37
Yosemite, 91, 94
YouTube, 88, 106, 134, 136
Yucatán, 24, 42
Yukon, 101

Zheng He, 90
Zimbabwe, 123
zoos, 53, 56, 66, 71, 78

183